FOCUS ON THE ERITREAN CONSTITUTION

A COMPANION TO ERITREANS ENGAGED IN
THE STRUGGLE FOR CHANGE

BEREKET SELASSIE

authorHOUSE®

AuthorHouse™
1663 Liberty Drive
Bloomington, IN 47403
www.authorhouse.com
Phone: 1 (800) 839-8640

© 2019 Bereket Selassie. All rights reserved.

No part of this book may be reproduced, stored in a retrieval system, or transmitted by any means without the written permission of the author.

Published by AuthorHouse 07/23/2019

ISBN: 978-1-7283-2003-8 (sc)
ISBN: 978-1-7283-2001-4 (hc)
ISBN: 978-1-7283-2002-1 (e)

Library of Congress Control Number: 2019910178

Print information available on the last page.

Any people depicted in stock imagery provided by Getty Images are models, and such images are being used for illustrative purposes only.
Certain stock imagery © Getty Images.

This book is printed on acid-free paper.

Because of the dynamic nature of the Internet, any web addresses or links contained in this book may have changed since publication and may no longer be valid. The views expressed in this work are solely those of the author and do not necessarily reflect the views of the publisher, and the publisher hereby disclaims any responsibility for them.

Contents

The Book's Three Parts: I II and III

Part I.   Introductory Discussion XI
   1. Focus on the Constitution and Paramount Values 1
   2. A Brief Review of the State of Disunity of the Opposition and the Need for United Action 11

Part II.   Two Interviews on Constitution Making in Eritrea 15
   1. Interview Between Bereket Habte Selassie and Professor Rich Rosen (1999). 17
   2. Interview Between Bereket Habte Selassie and Saleh Younis (2000). 58

Part III.   The Rule Of Law and Its Place in Eritrea's Agenda of Democracy Building and the Role of Parliament Under the Eritrean Constitution 121

PREFACE

The Constitution of Eritrea, ratified twenty-two years ago by a Constituent Assembly of the people, having been suppressed by the unelected President, remains unimplemented. It has thus been the subject of protests and a symbol of the struggle for change. In the recent wave of massive protests spearheaded by Eritrea's youth, the persistent demand of the Eritrean public has been immediate implementation of the Constitution together with delineation of the country's borders and release of all political prisoners.

Starting in April of this year, as an integral part of the continuation of the massive protests, a determined element of the Eritrean Diaspora initiated a program of regular and continual readings of each Article of the Constitution focused on the Eritrean Diaspora public in Europe, America, Canada, Africa and elsewhere in the world. This creative initiative helped in further mobilization of Eritreans thus proving that the Constitution is a potent mobilizing force. The said initiative has contributed to the education of the public on the contents of the Constitution. It was as a result of the inspirational aspect of this initiative that this author decided to produce the present book, which he termed a **Companion to the protesting public**. It is sincerely hoped that the book will help in encouraging more Eritreans and their supporters to continue in the struggle for Justice and Democracy. It is also hoped that the contents of this book, and in particular, the lengthy two Interviews, will help answer some of the questions lingering in the minds of a few Eritreans concerning the legitimacy of the Constitution.

I wish to thank my friends and colleagues, Professor Rich Rosen and Mr. Saleh Younis for the thoughtful questions they posed to me thus enabling me to provide additional thoughts to the origin and lengthy progress of the constitution making process and many of the ideas contained in Eritrea's Constitution. The two interviews complement each other admirably and will, hopefully provide rich material for researchers in the future.

The book Is dedicated to the courageous Eritrean youth engaged in the just struggle waged on behalf of their long-suffering people. May their courage and dedication be crowned with success soon.

PART I
INTRODUCTORY DISCUSSION

FOCUS ON THE CONSTITUTION AND PARAMOUNT VALUES

The constitution of Eritrea, which was ratified by a Constituent Assembly in 1997, has been suppressed by the dictatorial regime of Isaias Afwerki. Its suppression has meant the complete suppression of all democratic and human rights, making Eritrea the only country without a constitution in Africa and one of the few absolute autocracies in the world. Not only has the suppression of a popularly prepared and adopted constitution led to the imprisonment, without due process, of thousands of innocent citizens, including hundreds of prominent former freedom fighters who are languishing in prison incommunicado, but it has also enabled the dictator to rule as an absolute autocrat, destroying the economic and social base of Eritrean society. He has made decisions on war and peace singlehandedly without consultation with the people's representatives, or even his hand-picked members of his cabinet Ministers who cannot even ask questions.

It is, therefore, not surprising that the recent wave of popular protests calling for change, using the Slogan Yiakil (Enough) should focus on the constitution in their demand for change of regime. The constitution has become the number one topic of conversation and debate among Eritreans in the Diaspora throughout the world. Young Eritreans in their early twenties, who were not born when the constitution was ratified after a three-year popular consultation, are now in the forefront demanding that the constitution be implemented immediately to clear the way for regime change and the establishment of a democratic system of government. An active, and well-informed cadres of Eritreans are even organizing systematic readings of all the Articles of the constitution thus bringing to light what has been buried by the regime. In an extraordinary example of dedication and responsible initiative, the organizers of these series of readings of the Articles of the constitution has aroused enormous interest in the constitution, not only as a store of the fundamental values of the nation, but also as a symbol of unity, and thus a potent weapon of struggle for political change.

Paramount Values, Old and New

The reading of the Articles of the constitution has revealed to Eritreans who have been following the series of readings that what has gone wrong with their country is principally due to the suppression of the constitution, which means the suppression of the fundamental rights and freedoms that have been suppressed with it, and have led to the tragic state of affairs in which their people find themselves—politically oppressed, economically impoverished and socially desolate and disoriented with many families left without support.

In former times, even those, economically deprived and desperate, could rely on some modicum of safety network derived from the strong sense of family solidarity. People were not left to die of hunger. It is not generally known that there have been and still are "native born and bred" traditions of social values of freedom, dignity and responsibility that have been generally ignored or neglected. Elements of what we call Rule of Law exists in all the villages of Eritrea, the *Highi Indaba,* which contain customary laws (also known as native laws) that stood the test of time, even during the successive colonial rule, over which foreign laws were superimposed. The well-known Italian ethnographer and historian, Carlo Conti Rossini, has recorded in his writings the validity and general use of some of these customary laws by the inhabitants of the villages. Referring to them as guardians of village life, Conti Rossinin calls them ***guardia sens armi*** (unarmed guards). Most of his writings about Eritrean customary laws are contained in his seminal work ***Il Diritto Cosuetudinario dell"Eritrea***).

These customary laws are, for the most part, unwritten, though some attempts have been made in codifying some customary laws of Eritrea. It is argues by some writers that the fact of their not been written has advantages to the extent that they make for flexibility of interpretation which gives the village elders as custodians of these laws sufficient rooms in their application. Flexibility, i.e., the relative absence of rigidity is also one reason why customary laws have survived over centuries and in terms of the application their simplicity and absence of technical complexity makes them cheaper to utilize in litigation or arbitration. In village life, children are brought up being sensitive to the values of "native laws." As they approach maturity (ages thirteen to seventeen) village youth are expected to gain some knowledge of the main elements of their village laws, which they absorb by attending village assemblies *(baitos)* and court hearings, being attentive to what the elders say. The great Eritrean freedom fighter and one of the fathers of Eritrean independence (and the author's mentor) Mr. Woldeab Woldemariam has put on record that he learned not only local laws but also expanded and refined his knowledge of the Tigrigna language, of which he became a master, by attending village assemblies in the village of Ad-zarna in Serae province, where he grew up until age 17. The present writer had a similar learning experience though his experience was of a shorter duration, but long enough and intense enough to leave some lasting impressions about the importance of local laws and institutions.

One of the reasons for the limits of the applicability of customary laws was that its application was restricted to the village communities where it is observed. The circle of its jurisdiction was geographically delimited to a group of villages claiming a common ancestry. When Eritrea was declared a colony of Italy in 1890, the Italian colonial laws were proclaimed to have a common application throughout the colony. This was true with respect to criminal law and commercial laws as well as administrative law, leaving family matters to be determined in accordance of the local laws of the village communities.

One of the effects of colonial laws and administration was that the ideological and political hegemony imposed on Eritreans by their colonial masters—the market economy, the infrastructure, as well as the economic and commercial entities established by Italy—created a common sense of victimhood and shared destiny among Eritreans. Such common sense of victimhood and shared destiny eventually became the critical basis of their desire to resolve together to fight for self-determination and independence.

After half century of Italian rule, followed by ten years of British "care taker" administration and thirty years of Ethiopian occupation accompanies with thirty years of armed struggle, independence was achieved, and the in-coming government of Eritreans was forced to accept the *fait accompli* of colonial rule, just as other former colonized people of African countries had done. This meant adopting a set of national laws applicable to all parts of Eritrea with uniform application. Politically, also, whereas, in pre-colonial times, each region and local community followed and applied its customary laws, now a new and independent nation adopted national laws and institutions. The new national laws were applicable uniformly to all parts of Eritrea. The government began by applying Ethiopia's Code of Penal Law and Code of Civil Law, both Codes derived from foreign models, the first drafted by a Swiss Professor of law, and the second by a French Professor of law. The long-term project of revision of these laws has been under way and continues in circumstances of uncertainty and reluctance to abide by the Rule of Law.

Above all, the government suppressed the 1997 Constitution, and a new generation of Eritreans has started demanding vociferously for its implementation, as already noted. In what follows, we shall make references to some of the basic features of the 1997 Constitution, leaving reading of all its text to all Eritreans as their solemn obligation. It is hoped that such reference to some of the basic feature will stimulate Eritreans to read and become knowledgeable of their Constitution,

Basic Features of the 1997 Eritrean Constitution

The first feature is its brevity.

As the members of the Eritrean Diaspora who have been listening to the readings of the Articles of their country's ratified but unimplemented constitution will have realized, one of the distinguishing characteristics of the constitution is its brevity. Such brevity, which is also accompanied by clarity and coherence, implies that details are left for future legislation to elaborate. Brevity also means that all important principles governing the powers and responsibilities of government, on the one hand, and fundamental rights and duties of the people, on the other, are contained in the constitution, again with details of application of such principles left for future legislation to elaborate as the need arises.

This is surely one of its appeal, even for many foreign observers who have studied it, including those who witnessed the three-year process of its making (1994-1997). The advantage of the choice of a short constitution modelled on that of the United States of America is that it leaves details to be deal with by legislation. Why is this important? To begin with, if a constitution were to be detailed, every time that any part of a detailed provision written in the constitution needed to be changed, there would be constitutional amendment. This would lead to going through a lengthy and protracted process of amendment, which would imply difficulties of governance. A constitution is like an edifice constructed to last a long time, which is why amendment procedures require large majorities of the Legislature to pass. Now if the constitution is a detailed one, every time there is a need to make an amendment, it would be difficult to pass such an amendment. This is one reason why a short constitution is preferable.

That is why constitution makers are extremely careful in making sure that its content does not leave out any principles that are basic. As already note, this includes, on the one hand, all fundamental rights and duties of the people, and on the other, all matters related to the powers and responsibilities of the government. The text of most constitutions aims at striking a balance between liberty and security. In this respect, we need to draw a distinction between constitutions and constitutionalism. Constitutions are the written texts containing the basic principles pertaining to the powers and responsibilities of government, and the rights and duties of the people. Constitutionalism is the operation of constitutional principles as interpreted by the courts of law and applied by the other branches of government.

There is no need to give details of the contents of human rights. Two examples may suffice. The first concerns the principle of equality guarantee. In terms of this principle, all people have the right of equal treatment by the law. No person may be discriminated against, on the basis of race, ethnic origin, language, color, gender, religion, age, disability, political opinion, or social or economic status. This right is the foundation of democracy; in fact, it constitutes the unity of democracy and human right. Put another way, democracy is itself a fundamental human right.

The second example concerns the right to human dignity. According to this fundamental right, the dignity of all persons is inviolable, and no person may be subjected to torture, or to cruel and inhuman or degrading treatment or punishment. Moreover, no person may be held in slavery or servitude nor required to perform forced labor not authorized by law.

Human dignity is the aspect of human right that lies at the intersection of faith, law and morality. It is generally accepted now that religious belief supports commitment to a moral and legal regime of human rights, which is why many human rights NGOs are members of the faith community.

The Importance of the Role of a Court

It cannot be over stressed that the brevity of a constitution implies the importance of judicial power to perform the critical role of interpretation. In other words, the constitution provides for the need of an institution tasked with the judicial power of interpreting the constitution and other laws, including laws passed by all government bodies from the President down to the mayor of a small city or any governmental body. All powers of government and rights of people are thus subject to the jurisdictional authority of a court of law. In this respect the Eritrean constitution, like that of the United States gives the highest judicial power to act as judicial arbiter of rights and duties and powers and responsibility to the Supreme Court of Eritrea.

The Constitution provides as follows:

Article 48 -The Judiciary

1. The judicial power shall be vested in a Supreme Court and in such other lower courts as shall be established by law and shall be exercised in the name of the people pursuant to this Constitution and laws issued thereunder.
2. In exercising the judicial power, courts shall be free from the direction and control of any person or authority. Judges shall be subject only to the law, to a judicial code of conduct determined by law and to their conscience.
3. A judge shall not be liable to any suit for any act in the course of exercising his judicial function.
4. All organs of the State shall accord to the courts such assistance as they may require, to protect their independence and dignity so that they may exercise their judicial power appropriately and effectively pursuant to the provisions of this Constitution and laws issued thereunder.

ARTICLE 49-THE SUPREME COURT

1. The Supreme Court shall be the court of last resort; and shall be presided over by the Chief Justice.
2. The Supreme Court shall have:

    a. sole jurisdiction of interpreting this Constitution and the constitutionality of any law enacted or any action taken by the government;
    b. sole jurisdiction of hearing and adjudicating upon charges against the President who has been impeached by the National Assembly pursuant to the provisions of Article 41(6)(a)and (b) hereof; and
    c. the power of hearing and adjudicating cases appealed from lower courts pursuant to law.

3. The Supreme Court shall determine its internal organizations and operation.
4. The tenure and number of justices of the Supreme Court shall be determined by law.

ARTICLE 50 -LOWER COURTS

The jurisdiction, organization and function of lower courts and the tenure of their judges shall be determined by law

Other provisions of the Constitution in relation to the judiciary are:

Article 51: Oath

Article 52: Removal of Judges from Office

Article 53: The Judicial Service Commission

Article 54: The Advocate General.

Constitution, Democracy, Constitutionalism

As already mentioned, democracy is itself a human right, and the idea of constitutionalism is the golden line running through the relationship of democracy and rule of law. Put another way, constitutionalism is the soul of a constitutional democracy. It acts as a mediating principle between law and power.

So, what is a Constitution?

A constitution is a text embodying principles and modalities:

1. for the exercise of governmental power and for ensuring that governments are held responsible for acts and omissions, and
2. for securing the rights and duties of the people. A simple analogy is to compare it to the human body: the text of a constitution is like a body. Bu a body without a soul is a corpse, or a corpus, to use a Latin term, which needs an animus (a spirit or soul) to complete the essence of a functioning body. Constitutionalism is what gives the corpus meaning and life.

An eminent legal scholar has traced the origin and significance of constitutionalism as follows:

> Constitutionalism with its constituent concept of the secularization, nationalization, separation, and limitation of public powers emerged in Europe as part of the bourgeois revolution. The overthrow of temporal papal authority was engineered to bolster emerging national monarchies in Europe. The nationalization of power was necessary to advance the cause of national bourgeoisie in search of mercantilism. The other roots of constitutionalism are the need of capitalism for predictability, calculability, and security of property rights and transactions. Capitalism required the

conversion of serfs into wage earners and the expansion and consolidation of national markets, thus compelling the alliance of the bourgeoisie with the monarch against feudalism. Capitalism also the limitation of the arbitrary or discretionary powers of the monarchy (or the centralized state) against the intervention in property and contractual rights.

(Yash Ghai, The Theory of State in the Third World and the Problematics of Constitutionalism, in Constitutionalism and Democracy, edited by Douglas Ginsburg et al, at page 188).

The historical source of constitutionalism thus explicated in terms of the concept's link with the evolution of the political economy of Europe's capitalist market is perhaps the most accurate and satisfying narrative of this legal/constitutional concept. And we will leave it there.

A Brief Review of the State of Disunity of the Opposition and the Need for United Action

"The end is near, but are we ready for it?"

This is the question of the day all Eritrean opposition forces must answer…

…A few years ago, I published a booklet with the title *"While Waiting or Working for Change."* It was based on a Paper I presented at an international meeting of Eritreans, held in Pretoria, South Africa. Following my presentation and distribution of printed copies of my address, several participants expressed a wish that the speech be translated into Tigrigna and Arabic. Two people volunteered to do the translation, one in Arabic, the other in Tigrigna.

A few months later, Abdu Razag translated it into Arabic and **Samuel Bizen** into Tigrigna after which I approached Red Sea Press to publish it, and the Red Sea Press agreed. It was brought out in record time, and I am deeply grateful for Kassahun for his speedy work of publication, and for Abdu Razag and Samuel Bizen for their voluntary patriotic work in translating the booklet.

The booklet is available at Red Sea Press and, at my insistence, Red Sea Press made dozens of copies available for some leaders of political entities at least in a couple of meetings in America and Europe.

WHY AM I REFERRING TO THE BOOKLET?

Simply put, it is to remind all concerned the need for united action, which has become an Eritrean national imperative, more so now than ever before. The principal recommendation of the booklet was the need to establish a **United Front** of all the different political forces advocating or agitating for change in Eritrea. Leaving the detailed analysis made in the booklet for readers to peruse, it is enough for our immediate purpose to sum up the crucial point.

A United Front is suggested for two related reasons. The first and obvious reason is that without unity, there cannot be any regime change in the country. The choice of a united front, instead of complete unity is that a united front preserves the historical identity and integrity of the existing political forces, while ensuring a unified action to replace the dictatorial regime. Additionally, such a united front conceivably encourages the cultivation among all interested parties the need for establishing a multi-party democracy in the future, with the signatory members of the united front going their separate ways, following the change of regime, to be engaged in competition for political power under a democratic system.

As Saleh Younis, the astute observer and commentator, has pointed out in his foreword to the booklet:

"...It (the booklet) is not offering a blueprint for change as much as crystallizing the choices and making an argument for debate—but only within the context of a united front which he (the author) considers of paramount importance....We should step beyond *disunity, dissolution and vacillation* and approach the existential threat Eritrea faces decisively."

A Time for Urgent Action

Alas! Despite the call for confronting the "existential threat" facing Eritrea that Saleh alluded to, there has been no significant action taken by the Eritrean opposition political forces toward a unified action to bring about change. But events related to new developments in the region—in Ethiopia and Sudan—have created new momentum forcing the issue of a united action for change now.

Now, reports from within the country, communicated to me personally and shared with some individual leaders of the Eritrean media, indicates that there is a keenly felt general expectation from the people in Eritrea that the Diaspora political forces must be united and actually form a provisional government in exile. The expectation from such a government in exile is that governments in Europe and North America would support united demand for changing the dictatorial regime. The said reports coming out from inside Eritrea emphatically state that if such a united action among Diaspora political forces is proclaimed it would energize the dormant potential opposition inside the country and produce the needed movement and momentum for changing the regime. It would transform the wave of "Yiakil" (Enough) Slogan into concrete action and cause the massive involvement of young Eritreans inside the country in a sustained demand for change. While there is as yet no competed unity, nevertheless several opposition groups have recently decided to coalesce thus forming larger groupings and even attempting to create regional *Baitos* (Assemblies) representing regional Diaspora groups, in America and Europe. While this is promising, it does not meet the urgent demands being voiced by most people. One encouraging fact about these new developments is that the vast majority of the members of the groupings demanding for unity and reconciliation are younger Eritreans (from their early thirties to forties and fifties).

In essence, the objective of the demands being made by the groupings for a unity and reconciliation is another name for a United Front designed to form a united action to force the dictatorial regime out and to bring about democratic change. It is, therefore, possible that the opportunity missed earlier might be recovered. It is not clear to this writer why the older political group9ngs were reluctant to adopt the United Front idea, even from the standpoint of their corporate or group interest. Is it likely the idea of a United Front as spelled out in my booklet might be adopted as a shortcut for all the different demands being made by a different and younger groups? Time will tell. What is beyond doubt is that time and a younger generation of leaders are overtaking the older politicians whom seem to be stuck in the rut of old sentiments and indefensible fights and resentments.

PART II
Two Interviews on Constitution Making in Eritrea

Interview Between Bereket Habte Selassie and Professor Rich Rosen (1999).

COMMENTARY

THE ERITREAN CONSTITUTIONAL PROCESS:

AN INTERVIEW WITH

DR. BEREKET HABTE SELASSIE

Bereket Habte Selassie
Richard A. Rosen

Introductory Note

Early in 1994, almost a year after the Eritrean population voted overwhelmingly for independence, the Transitional Government of Eritrea issued a Proclamation, No. 55/1994, calling for the creation of a Constitutional Commission, and charged this Commission with the tasks of drafting a Constitution for the new nation and of organizing public partici

Dr. Bereket Habte Selassie is William E. Leuchtenburg Professor of African Studies at the University of North Carolina, Chapel Hill.

Professor Richard A. Rosen spent the 1995-96 school year as a Fulbright Lecturer in the Law Program at the University of Asmara, and is currently working as a consultant with the Eritrean Ministry of Justice on the revision of the Eritrean Penal and Criminal Procedure Codes. Special thanks are due Pat McKenzie of the UNC School of Law for her assistance with the transcription of the interview and Rebecca Slifkin for her patient and skillful editing.

pation in the drafting process. Soon after, in the spring of 1994, pursuant to this proclamation, a 50-member Constitutional Commission was named under the chairmanship of Professor Bereket Habte Selassie, former Attorney General of Ethiopia and Eritrean People's Liberation Front [EPLF] representative to the United Nations.

The Constitutional Commission of Eritrea, guided by a 10-member executive committee, undertook an arduous three-year process of Constitution drafting. The Commission set up two advisory boards, one of foreign constitutional scholars and experts and one of Eritrean experts on the nation's customary laws, and divided the constitution-drafting process into four phases. The first phase was largely devoted to procuring funding and organizing the Commission's activities. In addition, the Commission hosted a small "mini-international conference" and began to discuss a series of questions about the substance of the Constitution. The second phase, which commenced in December of 1994 and ended in August of 1995, focused on extensive public debate and education: it is estimated that more than 500,000 Eritreans, at home and abroad, participated in this phase of the process. A large international conference was held in Asmara in January of 1995, at which Eritrean and foreign scholars presented papers and held discussions on important constitutional issues. This phase culminated with the Commission adopting a set of constitutional proposals.

These proposals were subject to a massive public debate in Phase Three, with the Commission explaining and defending its proposals and taking detailed notes of the public response. The draft Constitution, which was released for publication in July of 1996, served as the basis for the fourth and final phase. After another round of public debate and education, the Commission met in February and March of 1997 and submitted a final draft Constitution to the National Assembly of Eritrea. This Constitution was passed by the National Assembly, and on May 23, 1997, it was ratified by a Constituent Assembly representing the Eritrean people. Thus ended a momentous three-year public process of creating a national charter for the new Eritrean nation.

The following is taken from an interview with Dr. Bereket Habte Selassie, the Chairman of the Constitutional Commission of Eritrea, conducted by Professor Richard A. Rosen of the University of North Carolina School of Law on July 9-10, 1997.

How did the process of creating the Eritrean Constitution get started, and how did you get involved in it?

Dr. Bereket: I became involved in the summer of 1993, when President Isaias asked me via the Eritrean office in Washington, by telex, whether I would be able to do it. Although I was willing and excited, and of course very honored, to be asked, I wasn't quite sure whether I would be able to do it in terms of getting the necessary leave from my University. I had long been involved in the Eritrean struggle in various capacities. Until 1991, the independence of Eritrea, I was the EPLF representative at the United Nations, which meant constant movement, constant travel, from Washington to New York and sometimes even to Geneva when the need arose, and that had made my home life difficult, and my income had stagnated. When I traveled I had to do part-time teaching or sometimes even take leave without pay. So I had to think very hard on how to go about this. When in July of 1993 President Isaias Afwerki formally asked me whether I was ready--he didn't even ask me if I was willing, but rather if I were ready to take on the task--I said, yes, I am, but on one condition--that he write a letter to the President of Howard University asking for a leave of absence for me under some kind of arrangement. He asked me to draft this letter, which I did. Upon my return to Washington in the Fall of 1993 I sent the letter from President Isaias to the President of Howard University. I also sent a copy of the letter to the Chair of my department, the African Studies Department. The letter also was sent to the Dean of Arts and Sciences, the College under which the department of African Studies came. The President of Howard University did not recognize the significance of this request, because not only did he not accept my request to see him and explain what I would be doing, he did not even take any personal interest in the matter. He sent the letter to the Vice President for Academic Affairs, who then sent it to the Dean of Arts and Sciences (who had already received a copy of it). I was quite astounded. I had to wait a month, by the way, before all this was revealed to me. So finally I had to go to the Chair of the department, and when I consulted with him he was very anxious and willing to help. In the letter that President Isaias wrote to the President of Howard University, it was suggested that should Howard University be willing to give me a leave without pay, arrangements for my pay would be made under the aegis of the Eritrean government, which would perhaps seek some funding from some UN agency or from other sources to fund my activities, so that there would be no adverse impact on my family, and would allow me to pay my mortgage and other expenses.

So there was a lack of interest on the part of the President of Howard University, the Vice President, and I suppose the Dean, because he did not want to see me either, or did not seek to see me. By that time I was quite outraged. I am spending a bit of time on this anecdote because it is important to explain why I left Howard University, where I had taught seventeen years, and then came to The University of North Carolina, which is another story. Anyway, when this didn't work out I resigned. It did not take long for me to leave Howard University, which shocked everybody, beginning with the Chair of my department and my colleagues. They were outraged, shocked, and they wanted to make amends, to help out. I said, No. There had been a complete lack of recognition of the significance of this letter by a President of a country to a President of a university. There was an absence of the simple courtesy even to acknowledge receipt of the letter and thank President Isaias for it, and nobody said "We are honored that one of our faculty is being asked to write the Constitution of a Nation." There was nothing, nothing whatsoever. That so outraged me that I did not even reconsider going back to Howard.

And so I decided to come to North Carolina. The University of North Carolina, if I may say so, a lily white University, was not only willing to accept my application to join the University, but they said, starting with the Dean of Arts and Sciences and the Provost at the time, Dick McCormick, that they were delighted, they were honored, and that this would be an honor to the university, and that they would consider leaning over backwards to help facilitate my going there. So I came to North Carolina in January of 1994.

How specific was the first approach from President Isaias? Were there any specific ideas about the Constitution mentioned?

Dr. Bereket: I remember asking him, is there any blueprint, or is there any idea of what the constitution is going to look like from the government's point of view or from the Front's [The People's Front For Democracy and Justice, or PFDJ, the successor organization to the Eritrean People's Liberation Front] point of view? Are there any guidelines that you would like me to consider, or even advise you upon? He said, "No, everything depends on you." I remember the words, it was ??? [*kullu kabakha'yu*]. Everything depends on you. I assumed that he meant this both in terms of the process of the constitution and in terms of the content of the constitution.

What was the next thing that happened?

Dr. Bereket: In between the time when President Isaias asked me to chair the Constitutional Commission, and the beginning of the Commission's work, there were several steps that had to be taken. First of all the members of the Commission had to be identified and appointed, which was of course a task of the government. There were several questions which I asked the President. Would I be allowed to choose some of the critical members of the Commission, some of those who would make up the Executive Committee? He said, "Yes, of course." I said as much as possible they have to be lawyers. We have very few lawyers and could only suggest those that are available, and he said "Certainly." This happened during his visit to the U.S. in September in the guest house where he was staying. I gave him a list of names of some seven lawyers. I also sent a couple of letters outlining my ideas on what needs to be done, and I was asked to draft the law that established the Commission.

Did you draft the law in English or Tigrinya?

Dr. Bereket: I drafted it in English and sent it to the President's office. It was translated into Tigrinya and then sent back to me. There were a few changes, particularly in the preamble, which had been longer in my draft. It was kept intact, practically, in all respects, except for a few details here and there--matters of style. So, I had to redraft the English--the English draft was mine--to take into account the changes that they had suggested and that I had made in Tigrinya. I also had to see that the Tigrinya wording was the exact equivalent of the English. That all happened in the fall of 1993, when I was on sabbatical leave teaching African history at Bowden College on the Talman Fellowship.

Can you say more about the selection of the members of the Commission?

Dr. Bereket: I cannot tell you exactly the process that was involved in terms of choosing the members of the commission. All of the nine officially recognized ethnic groups were represented, and religiously speaking it was almost half and half; Christians and Muslims, and of course there were the Kunamas, who are animists. The social and professional background of the Commission members is interesting. The majority were ex-fighters. I did not have any hand in choosing those people except to suggest that there should be some lawyers, and I gave their names, as I already said. With the exception of one person, all my suggestions were accepted. The others were chosen either by the Executive Committee of the PFDJ, or by a caucus of the President's office, or the Cabinet, let's say by the decision makers of Eritrea. I think they must have sat down and looked at the list of names to make it representative, because that's clearly a very important political decision. Who represents the nation that is going to draft a constitution is a critical political decision, obviously. So, it was a political decision which they had to make and they did make. Finally the list came out in the announcement, which came out in the newspaper. You could see that it was a body of people which represented a cross section of Eritrean society, as the law establishing the Commission demanded. It was required that it be composed of Eritreans who have made or can make contributions to their nation, representing a cross section of Eritrean society. That was the wording. I think that requirement was fulfilled.

How do you respond to the criticism that has been made as to the method of the selection of the Commission members, to the effect that if you truly want a democratic constitution, the people to be on the constitutional commission should be elected?

Dr. Bereket: This came up in several meetings with the members of the public, particularly abroad, among Eritreans in North America and Europe, and particularly from those coming from the former Eritrean Liberation Front [ELF], who are critical, of course, of the Eritrean People's Liberation Front [EPLF] and its government. They challenged the legitimacy of the Constitutional Commission on the ground that it was not elected by the people, as the former ELF people put it, that it did not take into account other political forces (meaning themselves). This became one of the bones of contention. We had to clear that up before we proceeded with the substance at all of our meetings. And my answer, my pat answer, was this. The government in place, the "facts on the ground," as they say, the government which won the independence for Eritrea--it's called the EPLF government. It's now the PFDJ [Popular Front For Democratic Justice]. This is a government which in our view--those of us who are supporters of the EPLF, or members of the EPLF --is highly representative of the Eritrean people, legitimate in any definition of the word legitimacy. This is a legitimacy coming out of a struggle, out of sacrifice--revolutionary legitimacy, if you will--in terms of changing the social structure and, of course, crowning it with the independence of the country. That government is perhaps more representative, or as representative, as any that I can think of. Therefore, a commission appointed by such a government cannot be questioned on the grounds of legitimacy. What the Constitutional Commission makes of its duties, of its function, is really the most important question, and how the public responds to its questions, how the public contributes to the task of constitution making, are surely the more important questions. I think most Eritreans were persuaded that this was so. So, my answer to the question is, simply, that election of a Constitutional Commission is one way. I didn't think the Constitutional Commission should be elected in the case of Eritrea because its task was to organize public meetings, hold consultations with experts, sound public views over a long period of time, gather facts together and then sit down and draft the best constitution possible, and then that constitution would be submitted to an elected body which would be a constituent assembly which would then either actually throw it out or accept it. Which is exactly what happened.

Another answer is that there were not many Tories present at the United States Constitutional Convention.

Dr. Bereket: Exactly. Let me take this opportunity to talk about the different approaches to constitution making. There are historically speaking two ways of constitution making. I call them the Philadelphia model and the Westminster model. The Philadelphia model is a peculiar one. It is based on a peculiar history of a nation, and it is of course classic, but it had faults, it had deficiencies, obviously. If it were to be repeated today, there would be an uproar as to its legitimacy, but it served for its time, for the purpose for which it was set up. The convention in Philadelphia came off with one of the best constitutions of the world, one of the best architectures of the human condition called governmental power. As good as any in mankind's history, I think, because there were assembled there some of the most remarkable human beings that ever came together, whatever their social class. It was the time of slavery, they assumed slavery would be a fact of life, forever. Nevertheless, what they came out with had to be then ratified by their respective legislatures, so that legitimacy was then taken care of by that fact.

The other model, the parliamentary model, the Westminster model, is a more practical one. Parliament was sovereign in British constitutional theory, so Parliament establishes a committee of Parliament, which is in lieu of a commission, to look at the facts in detail, to hold public meetings, to make consultations or investigations, and then to report back to Parliament. This has been tried, I think, in a few cases in the former British colonies in Africa.

Then there is the constitutional commission approach, which is now gaining ground, I think, as being the best. The constitutional commission approach has legitimacy aspects in terms of representation of the people, so that peoples' views will be represented adequately in terms of cultures, religions, ethnicity, and so on. A longer period of time is then conceived in terms of the debating that goes on. The commission then presents a draft constitution to a representative body, a constituent assembly. In our case there was the National Assembly in between, which sort of sifted, filtered, and submitted it to the constituent assembly––an approach, I think which probably will be a model for some time to come.

The Eritrean constitutional process appeared to be very self-conscious, that is, it appeared that there had been some thought about process before you started. Where did that come from? How did that develop?

Dr. Bereket: I think it developed as a result of two historical conditions. First of all the process in Eritrea during the armed struggle was a revolutionary process, which meant an elite group of people decided to sacrifice their lives if necessary to organize the public to liberate their country. They knew that they could not accomplish their task without involving the public. So, involving the public in the armed struggle became a critical element of the whole process, and a cause of its success. The public had been involved continuously, and increasingly more intensively, in the affairs of the nation as a whole. So, there is that historical background to begin with. The involvement of the public in discussions of issues of the greatest moment, like the constitution, is therefore something which had to be thought of as a first principle. The second source of this self-consciousness is perhaps a personal one, my own and those of my colleagues. The process has to be so well organized, and it has to be articulated so clearly, that the people are making their own constitution and, in doing that, empowering themselves. There is an element of self-empowerment in the involvement of the people in making their future constitution, and in this process of self-empowerment, perhaps I am exaggerating, you assume that a degree of control, sense of ownership of the product of the process, will be involved, and people will feel that in the future, if anybody tampers with this thing that they own, then they will take up arms if necessary.

Certainly they will, metaphorically speaking, take up arms, and there will be an uproar. So that this sense of consciousness is based both on the history of the struggle and on perhaps the felt need by myself and my committee, and of course with the agreement of the government, that the public must be involved concretely, clearly, substantially, and over a long period of time.

How did this consensus as to the process of constitution making come about?

Dr. Bereket: When we started the process on April 17, 1994, I had prepared a set of twenty-two questions which were culled from different constitutions I had read. I thought these were exhaustive questions which any constitution maker should ask. I chose this method and persuaded my colleagues that this is a better method of looking at things than proposing a model--American model, French model, British model, Tanzanian model, or Namibian model. These models we consulted in the future, after the first meeting, but we thought that the better method of looking at this thing, and the better method of involving, engaging the public, was just to list a set of questions. We eventually aggregated them into the most important fifteen questions, and then presented them to the public. This process of raising questions itself actually enhanced the inquisitive approach, and gave the public much more intensity, than if we had proposed a model, because a model carries baggage, a whole history and culture of the country from which you are taking it. So, you break it up, crossword puzzle-fashion, into questions such as "What form of government do you want?" "What is government?" "What types of government are there in the world today--republican, monarchical, parliamentary, etc.?" When the public debate began in earnest after January 1995, we were confirmed in our supposition that this would be a better method. As a result of the public consultation some changes were made. Some additions were presented to the commission, the larger commission, which accepted it. There was one additional question, added by the larger body, that there should be a separate question, the question of women--women's rights.

When did the executive committee first meet?

Dr. Bereket: In March, 1994, before the formal meeting of the Commission. We didn't have a headquarters, so we used the meeting place of the Municipality of Asmara. We met there two or three times, I think, and then we were given the premises which became the office of the Commission. Our first preliminary meetings were logistical. I had prepared a budget estimate of what needed to be done before I left, in the Fall of 1993, which ran to $4.3 million (U.S.), and the budget estimate had to be looked at by the executive committee. All the questions that I mentioned earlier on, all the related logistical questions about what needed to be done, had to be addressed. We had to decide what form of process of consultation to adopt. Eventually we had to decide on the international segment of the consultation. I explained to them some of the names of the scholars I had chosen, and these were cleared by the executive committee before they were presented to the larger body.

What was the next step in the process?

Dr. Bereket: We held a mini-international meeting in July, 1994. We didn't have money at the time so we agreed that, for the purpose of this sort of testing ground on how we think meetings would be useful to us, we would invite people who were available around the area who could pay for themselves. We invited two ambassadors: the Swiss ambassador, representing Western European nations, and the Namibian ambassador, to explain to us the developments in Namibia. We also invited the former chairman of the Constitutional Commission of Ethiopia and an Egyptian scholar whom the Egyptians paid to come, from Cairo University. Others were local people, our own intellectual resources.

The July meeting was with a limited number of foreigners and the full Commission?

Dr. Bereket: The members of the Commission who spoke English, because most of it was in English, were involved in the discussions, as well as other lawyers. The members of the Commission who did not understand English, of course, sat there, and people explained things to them. Those who were there participated during the question time. The meeting was open to the public. It was a very interesting experience. It was the first time, I think, for members of the EPLF veteran community, that such an open meeting was held in which the question of one party rule was questioned vigorously, and people, by implication, said that the EPLF actually should allow multi-party government. What was it doing ruling by itself? These questions, if not taboo, were not heard of. I remember a member of the EPLF, a young woman who was a member of the medical team who had just taken leave from her work, found it interesting. She said, "At first I was shocked, but then I said 'God, this is possible.' Then at some point I said, 'Is this real? What is going to happen to Bereket and his group. Will they be safe?' But by the third day, everybody was enjoying it. I said, 'My god, we are doing this.'" It was all worth it--the fight was worth it. That was the sort of feeling it generated.

Was there any debate on multi-party democracy at the beginning?

Dr. Bereket: In the January 1995 international meeting this question was one of the highlights of the debate. There was a very vigorous debate.

How was the international group chosen? And why was it chosen?

Dr. Bereket: We as an executive committee sat together and I proposed names, Paulos [Tesfagiorgis--a member of the executive committee] proposed names, and others proposed names. We looked at these. Additions and substitutions were made. It was a process of nomination which was consultative, more or less democratic, and some names were added because some of us did not know them. Ultimately it depended on what contributions they could make, and those are reflected in the papers they presented at the January conference. The criteria, the determining factor, was what contribution they could make and how representative they are geographically, professionally, and so on and so forth. A member of the external board of advisors, Crawford Young, a well known American political scientist and Africanist, has written about subjects like this over a long period of time, on multi-culturalism, on multi party systems, and so on. People like that were invited to come and make their contribution, people like Goran Hyden. Most of them happened to be Africanists, political scientists and lawyers, who have had experience in Africa, who had written about Africa, who had actually made a tremendous contribution. Some of them happened to be people who, like the former Chief Justice of India, I was sure would make a contribution, give us insights on what type of supreme court we should have. There was Mr. Laslo, the current President of the Constitutional Court of Hungary, suggested to me by Owen Fiss, the chair of the external board of advisors.

How long did the January meeting last, and what happened there?

Dr. Bereket: It lasted five days. The members of the international advisory board were invited to come to the January meeting, and we had funds by that time to pay for their trip. We had prepared what we called issue papers based on the twenty-three questions, which were aggregated into fifteen questions or so, the important issues around which were grouped a set of other, smaller issues. If we ignored other issues, that didn't matter, we thought. We drafted these issue papers as a Commission, proposing that this is what we think; that this is what a Constitution should be like. We sent it to the foreign advisers, and we asked for their comments. They made their comments in the January meeting. So, in a sense it was their meeting, but it also was a larger meeting involving other scholars.

Do you think the content of the Constitution is different because of the work of the foreign advisory board?

Dr. Bereket: Some of the suggestions made by members of our external board were very learned, very sophisticated, reminding us of mistakes to avoid, mistakes made by others. So, if not the actual text, content, of the main structure of the constitution, there was an effect at least in terms of some of the subtleties. Changes obviously were made in subarticles, wordings, or in certain concepts. In terms of the actual draft itself, it was informed by some of the insights defined in the papers presented, in the ideas proposed by people on the external advisory board and by the Commission members at the meeting in January. We made notes and among ourselves continually debated ideas, reminding us of what so and so said, what so and so wrote. It was a very interesting process of ongoing debate among ourselves, in our own minds, making references to these notes and these articles and eventually, of course, to the official recommendations of the international board of advisors. So that I cannot help feeling that we couldn't have failed to have been influenced in a subtle way by some of the views. But, the draft was ours. We drafted it. What ideas influenced it, our readings of history, and so on, is hard to say.

After the January 1995 meeting, what was the next part of the process?

Dr. Bereket: As a result of the overall outcome of the meeting in January 1995, we sat down as a committee, an executive committee, and discussed, what now? What have we learned from this meeting? What have we learned from the views of our advisors, or their views on our issue papers? We agreed to draft what we then called proposals. Before the meeting they were issue papers. Now they became the proposals of the Commission, based on our own earlier ideas, and the input of the participants in the January meeting. So, out of the January meeting came our own proposals as a Commission, which were printed as such, and submitted for public debate.

Beginning from January 1995 until the summer of 1995, we decided to instruct the public. We decided to hold what we call "civic education" with the public, a process which involved explanations of what the proposals meant, because the proposals involved intricate constitutional questions, like the judiciary's independence. By proposing this we were indirectly, at times also directly, asking people what they thought of it. We made notes, copiously. From January until May 1995 we made notes of these public education meetings, and took them into account in the executive committee's deliberations.

What happened next?

Dr. Bereket: The next phase, which started in the fall of 1995 and lasted until early 1996, was critical. In November of 1995 we met with our foreign board of advisors in Frankfurt. The reason we met in Frankfurt was that one of the board of advisors, Professor Simitis, who is a German professor in Frankfurt University, made arrangements for us to meet there, and the German government paid for the meeting. We stayed two or three days. We reviewed the proposals and the advisory board's reactions to the proposals. We sat and had very heated and frank meetings and discussions. Only three of the members could not come: two Sudanese, (one was sick, the other one could not get a visa from London to come there), and Professor Crawford Young, who sent his written views. The others came. We had a very, very good meeting. I remember some questions on women, for instance, being raised. One of our board of advisors members is a woman, a young American woman, Denise Morgan, who was a former student of Professor Owen Fiss. She is now a professor and is working on a text or article on Eritrea.

Based on the proposals and on the reaction to the proposals from our board of advisors as well as from the public, we sat down as the executive committee to write the first draft of the Constitution. The first draft came out early in the spring of 1996. Again, the public was invited to make their comments, to debate the draft.

Who was doing the drafting of the Constitution in the period after the January 1995 international meeting.

Dr. Bereket: All the time the executive committee was meeting, and we shared ideas. We discussed ideas. We shared opinions. But, ultimately someone had to do the draft, and that task fell on me.

Was the executive committee meeting regularly at that time? What about the full commission?

Dr. Bereket: The executive committee met regularly, but the full Commission met every three months, more or less. We didn't feel that there should be an assigned date for meeting because circumstances might cause us to change. For instance, we thought two years for the whole process would be enough, but it went eventually up to three years. On average, the meetings of the larger body were quarterly.

Who went out to conduct the public meetings?

Dr. Bereket: I should explain something here. In the Fall of 1995 we also organized a very critical, very important, little known meeting in the Sembel area, in what we used to call Expo, to which we had invited some 400 selected people. Their choice was of course done by consultation with the government, and the Front, and governors of the area who knew people who could be trusted to understand the main ideas of the constitution making process, the main issues that we had actually put into the issue papers, and eventually in the proposals. They had to be able to explain these things to the public after we gave them a kind of "training." The training was held for about a week in Sembel. All of us, members of the executive committee, and others like Kebreab [Habte Michael, a lawyer and member of the Commission], took part in giving lessons, so to speak. There were plenary sessions to which all the 400 were invited, and to which the members of our Commission were also invited, where we explained all the main tenets of what we thought should be explained to the public. Then we broke up into workshops, and all of us took part in explaining every section of the constitutional principles as we outlined in the twenty-three questions. Then we sent them to do their job.

Which was?

Dr. Bereket: Which was to organize meetings. Every member of the Commission theoretically had to go and explain, but there were not enough of us. We started with 50, but some people died, others were sick. We launched the meetings with members of the executive committee giving the main outline of the ideas contained in the proposals, and later on also in the draft, in the main cities of the then nine provinces. And then members of the Commission, and the 400 people who were trained, went down to the village level holding meetings. In the Spring of 1995, the second phase, which I characterize as a civic education phase, we reached some 500,000 people––half a million people in meetings, face-to-face meetings.

What happened at those meetings? Were you there in some of them?

Dr. Bereket: Yes I was. First of all, the meetings were organized with the help of the government in the locality, the administration there, and the Front of course helped, first of all, in the choice of the people. We established in each region a representative of the Commission. We had to have an office of the Commission, and a representative, whether he or she was a member of the Commission did not matter if that person comes highly recommended as a good organizer; someone who had a good sense of meetings, experience with meetings. That is where the experience of the EPLF comes in--in public meetings. First, to begin with, the representative had to know how to call meetings, how to identify people who are to be invited. He had to know the right people who will help him in doing that. So, we would call a meeting in a particular place in a city, city hall or cinema hall, and people who were considered to be the most knowledgeable, the most representative of the public, were then chosen and sent there. That's at the executive committee level. Then the real knowledgeable people of the village, the village elders, who on the whole turned out to be males, were sent. They would participate in village meetings, several times. We would begin with a general introduction explaining what the constitution making process involved, what the Constitutional Commission's mission is, what are the main issues that would eventually go into the future draft. The questions that we identified as being controversial, as being important, were contained in the proposals, and then questions arose from the public, on language, on customary law, the place of customary law there, on the question of women, on the question of religion, etc. All of this was recorded.

It seemed that in Eritrea there were two almost polar opposite approaches to the rights of women, the EPLF approach which was very interested in the liberation of women, and the approach of the traditional society, both highland and lowland, in which women were accorded a lower status. How did this come out at the meetings?

Dr. Bereket: We translated some eight or nine documents, mostly international legal instruments like the 1948 Universal Declaration of

FOCUS ON THE ERITREAN CONSTITUTION

Human Rights, and the international covenants that came out in 1966 on political and economic, social and cultural rights, and on women's rights, the resolution of the world convention against the deprivation of the rights of women. We ourselves issued a booklet on constitution making. We called it ??? ("*meba'ta quam*") in Tigrinya. We translated it into Arabic and Kunama and Tigre and other local languages. *Meba'ta quam* means "elements of the Constitution," or "introduction to the Constitution." That document was the one we used for the training in the Fall of 1995 for the 400 people. That became their quick reference book, a key to what questions they would expect and how to explain things. These documents were actually read over the radio all the time. I should have said that the radio was utilized to the maximum. In addition to the meetings, even while the meeting was being held, in anticipation of a meeting being held, we also used the radio in broadcasting some of these ideas. Editorials of *Haddas Eritrea* (the Eritrean newspaper published in Tigrinya and Arabic) were read over the radio, in Tigrinya and Arabic, in Tigre and other languages. From the very beginning, when we started the process in April of 1994, one of the most cogent, concise, and very clear statements on what a constitution means was the editorial that came out in *Haddas Eritrea*, and it was broadcast over the radio, powerfully, by some of the best known broadcasters, including a famous woman broadcaster. And so we had been preparing the ground, in sort of a multi-faceted operation: the radio, meetings, and of course the 400 people that we taught.

Now I made this introductory remark because in one of the documents, the question of women's rights, and the international convention on women's rights and the rights of the child, the whole question of democratic equality of men and women was articulated clearly, and openly, and loudly so that the public was prepared for that. Members of the public in the highlands, and several of the parts of the lowlands, did not even question it. In the areas where the struggle took place, in Sahel and other parts of Eritrea, women's rights, even among the conservative, especially Muslim elements, were not questioned, because women's rights were recognized--they have to be--the women fought for it. They won their place of honor. In some remote areas, however, even among members of our Commission, people raised concerns that this might not be appreciated. In the "Elements of the Constitution" we pointed out that in some areas of Eritrea women's rights were still not protected, especially in family laws, laws of inheritance, and division of property in the event of divorce. Some of the 400 people who gathered to be taught raised a concern that this might not be well-taken, this might not go down very well with some sectors of our community. Do we want to provoke them now? We said, we don't want to provoke them. We want to explain to them that Eritrea, as a member of international community, as a signatory of some of these conventions, cannot lag behind. So, we told them, in explaining this, tell them, please, that we do not want to disturb or upset the apple cart. We do not want to make people feel that we are here to abolish the Koran or the Sharia. The Sharia is part of the law. We recognize it and honor it. At the same time, there are aspects of practice, legal practice in the name of the Sharia, that go contrary to international commitment to equality, and contrary to our own commitment to equality and our revolution. Ultimately it will be resolved in the social struggle, in education, and in bringing these people to come to grips with this society. We cannot legislate or decree to a family in order to make women equal, but we can by example and by law and by practice and by teaching eventually convince them to accept it. In other words, it is a very difficult issue, and we cannot expect it to be resolved overnight.

What were the concerns you heard from people at the meetings?

Dr. Bereket: It's a difficult question to answer because there were so many issues that were raised. It depends on the area we are talking about. The main concern of people, a common denominator of concerns was that their religious practices, their favorite customs, customary laws, should not be disturbed. Sometimes this was articulated boldly in so many words. At other times they went about it differently, they listened to you, they tried to find out where you are heading. On the whole, the public, both Muslims and Christians, accepted the People's Front as their government and the Commission representing the Front as a legitimate, authentic body that was searching for ways of embodying in the Constitution their concerns, their interests. There was no question about that. In some of the areas in the lowlands, the main concern centered around this question of women. Some people thought we were trying to rob them of their right to control women. One Muslim friend of mine, an Eritrean, said, "Someone told me, 'Tell your friends they can do anything, but leave our women alone. Leave us with our women.'" It was said as a casual remark, and as a joke, but many a truth is said in a joke, and I told him "Well, it is a very difficult issue. We cannot decree equality, we cannot decree liberation, but we've shed some blood for it and I think they should appreciate that." And I told him, and I told some people, that perhaps one way that the government and the Constitution, given the conceptual and legal framework, can rapidly resolve this problem of inequality of women is to pass a law making elementary education for men and women compulsory. Assume such a law. Every parent would be required to send their daughters to school. Once those girls go to school, and start tasting the importance of education and share ideas and concerns with their men folk, by the time they are thirteen or fourteen, they will have reached a decision about how important education is, and how wonderful it would be for them to be professionals: doctors, lawyers, teachers. Then comes the secondary education. You may not make it compulsory, but then you begin to use persuasion, moral persuasion and other forms of persuasion, and that is the way, which involves social struggle of some kind. I think the People's Front is organized and able to do that. You then have a generation of women who will take care of the rest.

There has been criticism, primarily from Westerners, that all of this was just window dressing, a show to pretend that there was popular participation in what was really a top-down process. What do you say to that?

Dr. Bereket: I wonder what gave them that impression. Is it an assumption about Africa, about the Third World, including Eritrea, that it can't be done democratically? It has to be top-down? Or is it an assumption based on their assessment of the PFDJ as sort of a former Marxist government. This is not the first time I have heard it. I would ask the people who say this: Who organizes elections in America or in the United Kingdom or France? Do you leave it to the miner or the peasant and just wait because it is elitist to organize elections? Has that ever happened? Of course not. I would turn the whole question around. They are making such an assumption because they themselves are elitist. And then I would ask them to suspend their judgement, and give us the credit.

How could we have succeeded in a war when we were isolated, when we were all by ourselves, if we didn't have the support of the people? How could we have gotten the support of the people if we did not do something that was obviously to their liking? And I would also inject here a historical, cultural factor. We are talking about a very old society. A society that goes back thousands of years, that has had governance of its own kind, and laws that people do not assume away. People use language, symbols, which are critical. The first question that an elder asked me in one of the meetings was, "What kind of ??? ("*Luguam*") are you going to use to reign in the government?" "*Luguam*" is harness. He says, "*lugam*" is critical--tell me what kind of "*luguam*" you are going to have. He is talking about accountability. He is talking about transparency, in a local idiom. So we are talking about a society, a nation, that has laws, that has known governments, that knows what the rule of law means. I would answer such questions by asking questions in the manner that I did, and also by asking them to suspend their judgement and judge us by the results. And if they cannot, of course, then I wouldn't take their questions seriously.

When was the first draft prepared, was it the Spring of 1996?

Dr. Bereket: Yes. The first draft was really *the* draft, because the second draft which followed it had only minor changes. We knew it was going to be critical--*the* draft--and that is why we thought it was important to make preliminary preparations towards it in terms of issue papers, in terms of all the public meetings, the two international meetings, and the proposals that came out of the issue papers. The input was important in terms of making it really the critical draft. It was translated into

Tigrinya and it was compressed. Mine was a lengthier draft, and we went over it article by article for seventeen days, as a committee. What came out then was republished and submitted to the main Commission. A few changes were made as a result of the Commission's meeting, and then I sent a copy with my cover letter to the President. The President called a meeting of the Parliament, at which very few changes were introduced. This I think is a tribute to the systematic way, authentic way, that consultations with the public and the experts were organized.

What was your relationship with the government during this time-- 1994 to 1996?

Dr. Bereket: Minimal. I had meetings with the President on a couple of occasions, three occasions, I think, to ask some questions. Never to say, "What do we do?" Nor did he, at any moment, call me, even on the phone, to ask what the hell is going on or how are you doing or how far have you gone. Never. We held two or three consultations with the Front [PFDJ] leaders, to listen to the Front's perspective on how issues like language, the multi-party idea, the election, and other questions. If you hold consultations with the public, and with experts, you also have to have consultation with the party on which the government rests. It was always very useful. We sounded their views on certain ideas and they were very useful. There were some arguments on some issues. I would therefore say that the relationship between the Commission and the government was minimal; to the extent that we held meetings with them, they were useful--never confrontational.

How did the Commission resolve issues like whether to have a national language or whether there should be limitations on the number of terms the President could serve?

Dr. Bereket: That is one area where, I think, clearly consultations with the public and of course with the members of the government and Front and intellectuals became very important. We had to consider the views of such people. Take the question of language, for instance. Some of our members were of the view that there should be two languages,

Arabic and Tigrinya, as we had had in the Constitution granted by the U.N. You know, they are the languages being used now, the argument went, so therefore it makes no sense not to have them. On this issue we were persuaded by a very eloquently argued position by members of the Front, and members of the public, that to isolate two languages, as important as they are, and to make them official, or even working languages, would mean really going back on our word on the equality of the nationalities and their languages. The main identifier of an ethnic group is language. That is the window of its culture, its pride. If you don't recognize that, it is tantamount to not recognizing its equality. It was so powerfully argued that we accepted it, eventually. But many members of the public were not persuaded. Many members of the public thought that Tigrinya and Arabic should be the official languages, some said Tigrinya and Tigre, others said only Tigrinya, nobody said only Arabic, but there were variations on the theme of what languages should be official. Several people said that while we should not declare any language or languages official, since it is given that we have now Arabic and Tigrinya as the working languages, why not declare them as working languages? Eventually, the majority of people accepted the argument, which itself was accepted as a result of consultations, that simply declaring the equality of languages and letting history take its course as to which language will emerge is a better option.

On the question of whether to have term limits for the President, which, of course, is our proposal, the government, to our surprise, accepted the proposal without a word of objection. In the meetings of the Front, in our meetings with, consultations with people, some felt: Why should we limit ourselves? There is, for instance, the present President, and why should we deny him the service that the nation deserves from him? We said, well, we weighed two values on the scale. The value of having persons serve a longer time, not denying their service, is one side. More importantly, we think, on the other side of the scale is the idea of institutionalizing change, succession of leadership, and we also judged from the historical examples of other countries that one source of corruption and instability is the continuance in office of one person and his group. So that, in terms of avoiding corruption, in terms of accountability, in terms of really instituting a better democracy in our system, a term limit is critical. And the majority of the people accepted this, with joy. The question was whether Isaias and company would accept it. And we were all surprised to find that Isaias--a couple of members of the Parliament expressed reservations on a term limit--but Isaias was for it. And he articulated it in the manner I just articulated. Succession is very important, he said, and we should instill in our people the idea that nobody is indispensable, and that there should be succession.

Was there any thought of banning religious or ethnically based parties in the Constitution?

Dr. Bereket: Nobody to my recollection ever suggested it should be in the Constitution. Many people suggested, and indeed we included it in the proposals, that we should declare a secular state. That was declared, but we eventually thought it was wiser not to include it. We do have a secular state and will insist that we continue to have one, and if necessary laws under the Constitution can take care of it. The same is true with prohibition of parties based on ethnicity or religion. We shouldn't constitutionalize it, but it is something that can be taken care of by an ordinary law.

Which raises the question of the size of the Constitution and what its contents should be. We were faced with the question of whether we should make a detailed Constitution, or we should have a more concise Constitution, in the spirit of the United States Constitution, and then leave the evolution of other constitutional principles to judicial interpretation and to laws coming out of Parliament. We chose the latter option for obvious reasons. In my experience not only as a lawyer but as a practitioner in government, I had found that detailed constitutions tend to shackle governments. They tend to limit them. The details become knots binding them up. You would be facing problems that would be hard to solve without constitutional amendments. Whereas if they are in ordinary laws they can be changed a year or two later after trial and error. Amending the Constitution repeatedly to resolve problems would devalue the Constitution.

What about the very strong provision in the Constitution giving to the Supreme Court the ultimate power to interpret the Constitution? Was there controversy about that?

Dr. Bereket: The Constitution provides that the Supreme Court interprets the Constitution. The question of whether we should give this power to the Supreme Court rather than to a separate Constitutional Court was debated among ourselves and in the January meeting. The former Chief Justice of India and several members of that meeting advocated that we should have an ordinary Supreme Court as the interpreter of the Constitution. The current President of the Constitutional Court of Hungary and a few others argued for having a separate Constitutional Court, which would make the work of the Supreme Court, then, less critical. We opted for the American system for many reasons. One of the reasons was that creating a separate Constitutional Court is dangerous because once you put such an institution in place, it has to create a job for itself, and it might begin digging in and undermining the executive, and that would be contrary to our vision of a government with an effective executive but held in check by Parliament and also by a Supreme Court. So, for these reasons we thought that a Supreme Court was a better option. Once you make that choice, then of course you have to make the Supreme Court powerful, and the power to review the constitutionality of the actions of the other parts of the government is one of the powers. Maybe we have a tiger by the tail here. I don't know, but we will see. On the one hand we have a strong Parliament which holds the President in check, and I suppose also presumably through laws also holds the Supreme Court in check. But the Supreme Court, being the interpretive court, can actually throw out of court (no pun intended) a law passed by Parliament, which theoretically constitutes a limit on government. This is a critical part of the Constitution.

Was giving the courts this amount of power a matter of controversy?

Dr. Bereket: Not in our Commission, not at all. The literate members of the public wanted a more independent judiciary.

What about life tenure for judges?

Dr. Bereket: We left many details like that to legislation. I think it is wiser to leave them to legislation, so you can progressively tighten it and see how it develops. There is now a public perception that we have a corrupt and inefficient judiciary in place, and that tends to color the views on the future role of the courts, including the Supreme Court. We always try to make a distinction in people's minds between what should be in the future and what there is now. This was true in the case of arguing for a term limit. We are not talking about Isaias. Isaias happens to be a brilliant, charismatic, able, and dedicated leader. But Isaias is a human being with a life span, and we are thinking about a nation's life. After they heard this, people said, "Oh yes, o.k." The same is true with the courts, with the quality of the courts.

How much impact did the experience of other African nations and their constitutions have on the procedure?

Dr. Bereket: We looked at the models of Uganda, Ethiopia, South Africa, Namibia, and Ghana. The influence it had was in terms of enabling us as a committee to look at how other Africans dealt with making constitutions. In terms of influencing us in substance, not much. We did look at the Ugandan, Tanzanian, and Namibian Constitutions as kind of models to look at in terms of structuring the various chapters. We did find them helpful. The Ethiopian one being, of course, a federal constitution, did not help, because that is a different type of situation. Having looked at them as models, we then went about our job of finding an Eritrean model out of our own ideas and national experience.

What about the political experience in Africa over the last thirty years with constitutions and how they were ignored. Did that have an impact?

Dr. Bereket: It certainly did. In the process it did, in our own thinking, and in terms of insisting on a multi-party system. In terms of putting in the Constitution a provision that should give the right to form political parties, certainly. Because there were members who had strongly voiced views--this was from members of the public, and some members of the Front--there were those that said, "Eh, multi-party, oh look at Africa, look at Kenya, what's happening now. What we need really is an organized government, and we want to develop our economy." So, we had to resort to history. I personally have written a very lengthy pamphlet, which is also covered in a book, which explains this, in Tigrinya, with comments on Africa's experience, on one-party systems as one of the culprits for Africa's political debacle. Africa's one-party experience strongly influenced my thinking and my writings on this were distributed widely among the elites in Eritrea. Avoiding what happened in Africa over the last thirty years, and instilling the idea of multi-parties as a check on autocracy, on abuse of government's power--that certainly had an impact in our thinking, and therefore it colored the draft of the Constitution itself.

There was one current of opinion within the Front, that wasn't strongly voiced in the public debate, but you would hear it in the corridors of power and in conversations with some important members of the Front, emphasizing the need for guided democracy, saying that for a long time to come we need to have one party. Including multi-parties in our Constitution, the argument went, is something that will tie us down. Our answer, of course, had to be based on the history of Africa. In that sense, therefore, in terms of convincing important members of the government who would have a voice in accepting or rejecting the draft, we had to have an intellectually and historically based argument in favor of whatever proposals or draft we put in place.

When was the major draft done?

Dr. Bereket: That was done in the Spring of 1996, and it was adopted by the Parliament, if I am not mistaken, in June or early July of that year.

What do you mean by adopted by the Parliament? What did that entail?

Dr. Bereket: The Constitutional Commission was established by a law, Proclamation number 55/1994, which required that the draft be submitted by the Commission to the present Parliament, at the time the Transitional Parliament. And then the Parliament would approve it. The approved draft would then be submitted for discussion to the public.

Were any changes made to the draft in Parliament?

Dr. Bereket: Very few changes. One was on women. Our draft was weaker on the rights of women, but Parliament made it stronger. There was a debate within our Commission as to whether we should in fact have an article specifically mentioning women's rights. One school of thought within the Commission, the majority in fact, was that if we speak about human rights as a whole, and we have an article in the Constitution which specifies that the use of the masculine gender in the Constitution applies to the feminine, that should take care of it. To isolate the women question and give it a specific article would in fact derogate from the importance of the rights of women, making them a special case. Since we accepted equality, why should we then make an exception of them? If we do that with the question of women, then we have to do it with the children, the handicapped, the aged, with any number of other questions. That was the majority view. A minority view had insisted that, no, we should have an article on women. So, there was a compromise article, which in the draft spoke about the importance of taking the culture and tradition of the country into account, and therefore requiring the Parliament to pass laws that would address the question of inherent inequality, or words to that effect. And the Parliament stated, "No, they should actually have a stronger right, providing that discrimination against women would be prohibited by law." The equality principle among Eritreans is one of those things that cannot be suspended. It doesn't specifically say women, but it says equality among citizens will not be suspended under any circumstances, including a state of emergency.

After the Parliament approved the draft, what was the next step in the process?

Dr. Bereket: The next step was for us to take the changes made by Parliament into account and put them in the draft. We had to re-issue the draft, circulate it among the public, and then the public would debate upon it. The debate on the first draft was much lengthier, much more involved. There had been more outpouring in the public debate at the earlier time than in the second debate, because we were now treading familiar ground. There were some questions, including women's rights and others, that were repeated. So that the debate on the adopted draft, although it was important, was not as important as the debate on the first draft. It allowed the public and us, I think, to revisit some issues, because we did not want to limit people, to focus attention only on the changed articles. We gave them, in other words, another opportunity to revisit the entire spectrum of issues contained in the draft, so that it gave us an opportunity to look at the draft again as a whole, not just at isolated articles.

Was the discussion different in any significant respect?

Dr. Bereket: I wouldn't say so, no. There was repetition. It gave people an opportunity to revisit issues, and people who had re-thought their position on some aspects of the previous draft, individuals, for instance, among the educated elite, made contributions. Some of them sent written views, detailed commentaries on some aspects of the Constitution. Otherwise, as far as the general public was concerned, there were not much change. No new ground was covered.

Was anything changed between the draft that came out of Parliament and the final product that you presented?

Dr. Bereket: There were a few changes. One of them, in my view the most significant, was that we decided to add the position of the Attorney General, which we now call the Advocate General, so that the chapter on the judiciary has one additional article. At one point three of us were summoned to the Parliament to explain certain articles of the draft and, at the end of our explanation, we raised the question of the Attorney General or Advocate General, ??? ("*Akhbar Higghi*")--in Tigrinya it is the same thing. I explained to them the difference between the American system and the European system. The President, who was presiding over the Parliament, said: "Thank you. We'll consider it, and will discuss this question with the appropriate Ministry, and we will get back to you." They didn't get back to us, either because they didn't discuss it, or maybe because it was forgotten. So we took the initiative to take it up again, and then insisted on including it and it was accepted.

What is an Advocate General?

Dr. Bereket: In the British system you have an attorney general, or in the continental, Italian, French system, an advocate general, or procurator general, as they call him in Russia. There is a long history of this office under monarchical systems. In Italy, for instance, they used to call him the *"procuratore del Re,"* the "King's procurator." He was in a sense insulated from the daily pressures of particular governments. He was the king's procurator, therefore by extension the people's procurator, because the king represented, ideologically, theoretically, anyway, the nation. There was a sense of the procurator general, the advocate general, being an independent office, independent from political pressures, in terms of deciding whom to prosecute in criminal cases and whom not to prosecute, and in terms of advising on certain issues to the government. The American Attorney General is a political office. The Attorney General is the Minister of Justice, and is also in charge of the FBI. In the British and continental system, the advocate general is or can be the main legal adviser of the government, the advocate for the government, but at the same time he is in charge of prosecutions. He decides whether to prosecute or not to prosecute. Eritrea has followed the British system.

Is the Advocate General part of the Ministry of Justice?

Dr. Bereket: Yes, he is part of the Ministry. The Advocate General is a hybrid institution. It has a judicial, or quasi-judicial nature, and it also is in the executive branch, because the President appoints him or dismisses him. Once appointed, however, he can't be dictated to, by anybody, concerning whom to prosecute or not to prosecute.

The Minister of Justice would not have that power?

Dr. Bereket: No, the Minister would not have that power. Let me explain. I am glad you raised this, because it is an issue of which I have some expertise. I was, after all, Advocate General of Ethiopia. That was not the Attorney General in the sense of the United States, but the Advocate General in Ethiopia, Attorney General in Ethiopia, as I just described it. There was a Minister of Justice who was just a political minion of the Prime Minister or the Emperor, but the position of the Attorney General in Ethiopia was the principal legal advisor, the person in charge of the prosecution branch, and at the time when I was the Attorney General, the person in charge of the administration of criminal justice. Eventually we adopted the position of having an article on the Attorney General, or Advocate General, in our Constitution.

When did you prepare the final draft of the constitution?

Dr. Bereket: In the Fall of 1996.

What was the process after that?

Dr. Bereket: It was the same process. The executive committee met. The time it took us was much shorter than the previous time, because we only had to consider the changed articles or the new articles. I think we did it in a couple of days--two or three days. Then we presented it to the final meeting of the Commission, the full body. It was approved, and then we sent it to the Parliament, and to the President.

Did the Parliament then make any more changes?

Dr. Bereket: No.

And then it was sent to a Constituent Assembly. How was the Constituent Assembly constituted?

Dr. Bereket: There is a law which required that it be composed of present members of Parliament and all the members of the newly elected

Regional Assembly, all of them, so that popularly elected people would be members of the Constituent Assembly. The other option was to elect people specifically for that purpose. The government said, "Why the need of another election? They are elected, they are the best available." If you have to have another election, the second best would be constituting the assembly. We accepted that.

There was another element in the Constituent Assembly--the seventy-five members of the diaspora. So you have seventy-five members of Parliament, seventy-five members of the diaspora, and some 300-odd people, the elected members of the Regional Assembly. They all came. They all gathered together. We did not attend that meeting. The President addressed the assembly, and then got off the podium. I think he sat among the members, and the Secretary General of the Front asked the members of the audience how to appoint the Chairman of the Constituent Assembly, because the law says the Assembly appoints the chairman. And then they appointed a high ranking member of the Front--and he, then, asked the Assembly to elect a secretariat, and then the meeting was held for two or three days.

Were there any further changes made by either the Parliament or the Constituent Assembly?

Dr. Bereket: Very few. Nothing was communicated to us in writing, but orally, we were informed that the changes were on the privileges and immunities of Parliament. We had provided that members of Parliament would be immune from criminal prosecution during the session of Parliament. The Constituent Assembly said, "No they should be immune throughout the life of the Parliament, five years," which was very interesting.

What did you do? Was that changed?

Dr. Bereket: What could we do? Our task was done. Our task was finished.

Did they change it?

Dr. Bereket: Oh yes. That was the only thing I know of. There were some other minor changes, really detail, matter of wording, just stylistic. Otherwise, in substance, they didn't change anything. It's interesting, though, for the Constituent Assembly to insist that for the members of Parliament the privilege of immunity should be extended throughout the five year period. This reinforces our demand, throughout the three year process, that Parliament should be regarded as a very important institution. It also depends on how many months in the year Parliament will assemble. If it is going to be assembled according to the rules which Parliament itself will make, only say three or four months over the year, then this privilege is going to be extended over a period of time during which they will not be doing the business of Parliament. This I think would be very problematic. It would raise questions from the members of the public. But we will leave that up to the future.

How is this all being implemented now?

Dr. Bereket: I don't know. The Constituent Assembly, by the way, appointed seventy-five members of the Regional Assemblies, and fifteen from the diaspora, which makes ninety, and the members of the Front, to constitute the Transitional Parliament. So, there is a Transitional Parliament which will put into effect the requirements of the adoption of the Constitution. That was foreseen and provided for in the law establishing the Constituent Assembly. So, you have now a Transitional Parliament which will be, among other things, passing a law on elections, an electoral law, including establishing an electoral commission--that will be the first task. The next thing is deciding when and how a Parliament is going to be elected. That's important.

There are questions about the present press law, and the anti-corruption law. Will they survive the enactment of the Constitution?

Dr. Bereket: The attitude of the government towards the Constitution has been one of respect, that there is no other alternative, and this was made clear throughout the debate. People raised the question of the emergency anti-corruption laws in the courts, about the absence of appeal, which would be unconstitutional. I mean, with the Constitution--it would be unconstitutional. One person told me, "Supposing the President in violation of the Constitution insists on holding that court?" I said, "Well, the President would then be acting unconstitutionally." "What would you do with him, then?" "He would be impeached."

If the Constitution had been made to come into effect on May 28, 1997, there would have been a government which would have been acting in violation of the Constitution in these areas. Because of our awareness of this, my advice had been to say, there are two ways of taking care of this. If you still need time to clear the deck in terms of these new courts established to fight corruption, then you can extend the date of the Constitution coming into effect until January 1998. Or you can extend the date or clear the deck before that. Since it was not possible to clear the deck, the establishment of the Transitional Parliament would deal with transitional provisions. So, there's a Constitution whose effectiveness is suspended in the air.

In terms of the goals you set at the beginning for the constitutional process that you talked about earlier, how would you evaluate what happened?

Dr. Bereket: The Charter of the People's Front for Democracy and Justice, which was a well articulated, clear, concise, statement of the vision of the Front, was a very important point of departure for us, in terms of acting on what we considered to be a national consensus as to what should be done. There were habits of doing things, habits of the past, and there was a vision of the future. As always, of course, there was a contradiction between the two, and the Constitution is in between. The Constitution is the framework by which you break out of the past, or change the past and go forward into the future. What the Front's Charter did was to articulate five major goals or values to guide the Front, and the future of the country. We had that as our point of departure for the debates. We developed it, we articulated it, differently, but those are mainly our beginnings. First of all, the question of national unity and stability is a very important value. Without national unity there can be no civil order. If there is no civil order there cannot be democracy or development--I don't think it is in dispute at all. And, secondly, with regards to democracy, democracy is a very much bandied-about word, we can spend hours debating about what we mean by democracy, but I think there is a universal acceptance of what are the main tenets of democracy. It's obviously the preeminent political value of our epoch, for over 200 years. How we go about it, the so called democratization process, for instance, assumes certain things. Is electoral democracy the only thing? Is there something more important than that? These are points which we debated extensively within our Commission and with the public. And they are in the proposals itself, this notion of economic democracy being an important element of democracy, a different dimension of procedural democracy. These are developed in the proposals, and this comes from the Front's point of view, which we shared and developed. And then there is economic development, as policy and practice, as a necessity for a nation--you have to have development. You cannot distribute what you do not have, so you have to develop. Economic development is a very high priority of the government. How you go about economic development, and achieve optimal results without disturbing a great deal of other values is a critical question. What policies you follow, is it going to be a statist driven policy or are we going to give maximum leverage to the market? These are debatable issues. We did not want to include these things in the Constitution, but there are elements of the policies on this included in the Constitution, what the government and state is required to do and what the public has to do in this respect. Then there are human rights, and there is social justice, social justice in terms of the provision of the necessities of life, education, food, health, employment, even clean air these days. All of these cannot be put in the Constitution in detail. Our view was that you should not put into the Constitution what you can't fulfill. We decided to put the bare minimum principles there, and leave the implementation to legislation. These are important starting points for us. I expected some opposition parties, somebody to come forward and say: "This is a vision I don't share, or I oppose, or I challenge, therefore I have a different vision." None was forthcoming in this respect. We expected people, the ELF people, to say, "No, I do not accept this part of the EPLF's vision, or value or goal." Nobody did.

They never articulated anything even in opposition?

Dr. Bereket: They never articulated anything, in opposition to it or challenging it or in any way wanting to qualify it. We concluded from that, early on, that there was a national consensus based on the Front's charter, which everybody, even the so-called opposition, accepted. We decided this was actually a very important basis of consent to go forward. We felt that we were justified in going into detail, breaking down the principles, and then asking for people's comments. I would say that we may have stumbled here and there in the beginning, but by and large I think both the method we adopted, the time it took, the four phases, and the things that we did throughout the four phases, were done the right way.

What about other criticisms you've heard of what you have done, either from Ethiopian intellectuals or ELF?

Dr. Bereket: I haven't heard any criticism from Ethiopians. Some people have wondered why we didn't have a popularly elected Constituent Assembly. Why use the regional assembly which is filled with Front's people anyway? Why not let the public choose? My answer to that is, how do you know that these people were selected by the Front? These are people who were elected on the basis of fair elections, and I followed some of them, and some unexpected people were elected in some constituencies where they were not born, because of their character and record. The best people, the best available were elected and therefore we thought the government's choice of using the Regional Assembly is more effective, actually, because it represents the best available in the country. There are many different ways of democracy. If you restrict the definition of democracy to a formalistic approach of universal suffrage, election according to certain formulae, that I think is a mistake. Other criticisms from the ELF were on the "legitimacy" of the Commission at the beginning. They wanted the Front to consult them, as a body, and to ask them to send representatives.

Didn't the Chamber of Commerce have a representative on the Commission, as well as the various nationalities?

Dr. Bereket: All of them were included.

Was there at least a ceremonial role for the Grand Mufti and the Patriarch of the Coptic Church?

Dr. Bereket: Not in the Commission. They were never represented on it. One of the most remarkable things that I discovered was that the high ranking members of the Islamic community, beginning with the Mufti, a very intelligent and highly educated person, by the way, were actually more articulate than some of our members in terms of explaining why Eritrea had to have a secular state. The history of Eritrea over the last forty, fifty years, the inter-confessional strife is well known, at least at the beginning. At the time of the British there was Islamic-Christian based strife which was provoked and fostered by Ethiopia, but our common struggle corrected that. What the struggle taught us was that we are here to live with each other, among each other. It taught us that a nation like Eritrea, a small nation more or less evenly divided between the two religions, can't afford to have any political movements or parties organized along religious lines. It would be fatal. The Mufti used the word "suicidal," actually. We didn't need to convince anybody among the religious communities, Christians and Muslims, that a secular state was a necessity. How you articulate that in the Constitution is a different matter. On one occasion I actually invited the Mufti and the Primate of the Eritrean Orthodox Church, and the Protestant and the Catholic leaders to my office. Just, first of all, as tradition requires, to ask them for their blessing, for their prayers; and secondly, to assure them of two things about religion. One, we are a nation which, being divided half and half into Muslims and Christians, has to maintain the equality of the two peoples following the two religious faiths. There is a fundamental human right to religious freedom, and that is going to be an article in the Constitution. There is no question about that, that's the first point. The second point, I told them, is that we will not confuse or mix religion with politics, so there is going to be a secular state. And everybody without question accepted that.

FOCUS ON THE ERITREAN CONSTITUTION

Have you had any international response to what happened, to the process, any praise or condemnation?

Dr. Bereket: I have received several laudatory remarks from the Ambassadors as they came to interview me, or as I met them in receptions. I have talked to people in Europe throughout my travels, people in government who told me some nice things about how much everybody is talking about it. I have not heard any written statements to that effect from anybody, but I don't know, who knows? I think the American ambassador had written to that effect. I haven't seen it. It is of course classified, but I had heard that he said the most wonderful things about it as a model for Africa. I think the word is out that it is a successful constitution making effort, that it was fairly well planned, conceived, and executed, and that it was independently organized and executed, that the government kept its hand off of it, and that the chairman and members of the commission were satisfied as to that.

How was the constitutional process financed?

Dr. Bereket: The government gave us the office, and they gave us money to start us off because there was no money when we started. The fund raising campaign took place between April and December of 1994, but until December of 1994 we didn't have any money coming in. The Americans made the first commitment of half a million dollars. I traveled to Washington in late May, early June, and met the number two man at USAID, who immediately made a commitment for half a million. His name is Dick McCall, and he was chief of staff of USAID. He said that this is going to take time, but we will commit half a million dollars, and this was advertised appropriately and the U.N. followed suit, and the Europeans and others. There was no problem with money.

Were there any attempts to exert control over that money?

Dr. Bereket: None whatever. There was a request for a report of what was going on, of course, which we supplied verbally. And some of them wanted it in writing: we told them they had to wait, and we sent them the necessary report in time. The European community, for instance, was very eager to have their name mentioned, how much they contributed and so on, which was done in time. Otherwise, it was very smooth sailing.

Where are all of the Commission documents?

Dr. Bereket: One of our last decisions as a commission was to decide what to do with the documents. Our earlier understanding was to pass them on to the law school, but there is no physical facility in the law school so they are housed in the Center for Documentation--the center for research and documentation of the Front in Asmara.

If you had sat down with your executive committee and the Commission in 1994 and written a constitution in six months, do you think it would have been different than the constitution that came out?

Dr. Bereket: Oh yes. I can tell you without any hesitation whatsoever that the actual draft Constitution, the actual Constitution, would have been much different if we, I and a couple others, had just sat and drafted it in sort of ivory tower fashion.

Looking back, is there anything you would have done differently as far as the constitutional process?

Dr. Bereket: No, I don't think so--maybe there are matters of detail, matters of organization, but nothing really of substantive importance. I wouldn't have done it any other way.

Acknowledgement

We wish to acknowledge at the outset the shortcomings of this interview--it was originally not intended for publication, but instead was to provide background information for an upcoming analysis of the Eritrean Constitution-drafting process in the North Carolina Journal of International Law and Commercial Regulation. Thus, it does not purport to give the reader a comprehensive overview of the constitutional process, and it may at times assume more knowledge than some readers have. We hope, however, that this interview will provide some insight into the process for the reader and, further, that it will be useful to historians and others interested in this important epoch of Eritrean history, and will help begin the process of creating a historical record of the Eritrean Constitution-drafting process.

2

Interview Between Bereket Habte Selassie and Saleh Younis (2000).

Eritrea Digest
<u>PULSE</u>
On Eritrea's 1997 Constitution

Posted On May 29, 2019

This interview was originally published by <u>awate.com</u> on February 28, 2001. It was continuously updated to include follow-up questions by the interviewer and in response to readers' questions, posed directly to the *interviewee, until May 17, 2001. This will be first in a series of research documents on Eritrea which will be published in this "Pulse" column.*

Context: at the time this interview was conducted, a committee chaired by Mahmoud Sheriffo (G-15, disappeared since) had drafted a law on party formation and the National Assembly (since dissolved) had announced there would be national elections in December 2001.

Awate.com Exclusive: An Interview With the Principal Drafter of The Eritrean Constitution: Dr. Bereket Habte Selassie

Interviewed by Saleh Younis, February 28, 2001

A man of unique credentials and one of Africa's few constitutional scholars, Dr. Bereket has played prominent role in the recent histories of Eritrea and Ethiopia. This unique training and willingness to serve has seen the chapters of his life unfold from Ethiopia's Ministry of Justice, to Ethiopia's University, to the Commission of Inquiry investigating the offenses of his former employers, to the Eritrean field, and to the UN as Eritrea's Representative, to chair the Constitution Commission of Eritrea (CCE) and, finally, a citizen who, as member of "G-13", helped articulate a view of advocating the immediate implementation of the ratified constitution he was instrumental in drafting.

Given the subject that is going to be covered at some length—the constitution—and its importance on Election 2001, we expect and we welcome our readers to ask Dr. Bereket questions—especially those we haven't thought of. This, then, will be an "interactive" interview and we ask readers to mail their questions to DBHS@awate.com.

Part One of the interview will offer a brief background of Dr. Bereket as well as touch on the make up of the Constitution Commission. Part 2 through Part 4 will deal with specific articles of the constitution. Part 5 will deal with the writings of Dr. Bereket particularly those posted in the Eritrean websites. The final part, Part 6, will be answers to questions posed by readers.

PART I

Could you tell us a bit about your background?

I was born in the suburbs of Asmara, before the defeat of the Italians by British and Allied forces. I did my elementary schooling in Asmara and Harar [Ethiopia], my secondary education at the Wingate School in Addis Ababa; and my university education in England (LL.B. and Ph.D. in law; 1967.) I did my post-graduate research/study in the United States (1964-65). Between 1949 and 1957, I also spent some time in France and Italy, studying the languages and literature of the two countries.

My education being in law, I was posted in the Ministry of Justice in Addis Ababa upon my return with my first degree, and was eventually appointed as Attorney-General of Ethiopia and held other positions. In 1963, following the abolition of the federation between Ethiopia and Eritrea, I sought to resign from my duties as Attorney General. I had expressed disagreement on the imperial government's policy and action regarding Eritrea and things came to a head when the Emperor abolished the federation. The request was denied, so I had to wait for an opportune moment, seeking a way. The opportunity came in 1964, when I applied to and was accepted by the newly established Law School at Addis Ababa University as a lecturer in law. Before I could start teaching, however, I managed to secure a visiting fellowship at the UCLA Law School in 1964-65, so I quietly left for the United States without the permission of the Emperor.

You mean you need permission from the Emperor to leave the country?

If you are an Imperial appointee, you cannot leave without Imperial permit. It is what they call *les majeste*. And *les majeste* is a criminal offense: a crime against the king.

So you committed a crime against the king?

Oh, yeah. Big time. This was tantamount to treason and was one of the reasons for my subsequent troubles with the Emperor. Immediately upon my return from abroad, the Emperor banished me to Harar. When I joined the revolution, you know what the Americans called it? A lawyer-turned-outlaw…

Not a harsh punishment for something "tantamount to treason." For the emperor not to punish you, it must be because you had family connections, nobility…

Oh, no; I am the son of a simple peasant. I had a certain reputation amongst colleagues, most of the progressively inclined, liberal elite. He was a clever man. He never went out of his way to harm anyone or do anything against someone who is popular. If it had been Mengistu, I would have been shot summarily. Had it been 30 years earlier, the Emperor would have sent me to some remote land in chains, what they called *yegir bret*. But by then, he was worldly, wiser. My punishment was to be banished to Harar.

When was this?

That was in 1967 as the Eritrean Liberation Front (ELF) was stepping up its attack against Ethiopian security outposts and on government personnel. The crimes of which I was supposedly guilty was to belong to the Jebha [Front], as they called it, and that I was one of its leaders. Of course I was not one of Jebha's leaders; I didn't even belong to any liberation organization in any way, shape or form at that time. I had sympathies to the ELF, like most Eritreans at the time and I had briefly belonged to MaHber Showate [*Cells of Seven*, also known as *Haraka* in Arabic and the "Eritrean Liberation Movement" or "ELM" in English]…

You briefly belonged to Mahber Showate?

Yes. A disastrous organization! So ill-organized, people were boasting and recruiting openly, and the police would follow us everywhere. That is how most people were caught. The movement in the lowland— the *Haraka*—was better organized. But we were in the belly of the beast. Fortunately, the Chairman of our seven-member cell was able to contact the superior. Only if the chairman is caught is there real danger. Fortunately for me, the chair of my cell was not caught.

And who was that?

Yohannes, happens to be a cousin.

Did your name make it to <u>Nawud's</u> book [a chronicle of the *Haraka* movement]?

I doubt it. Because the connection between the lowland and highland was rather loose. The *Haraka* movement continued separately. I doubt it….When we [Nawud and Bereket] met in Beirut in 1975, we discussed it and we had a laugh. There was no discipline…that is what led to the collapse of the underground.

This was in Addis?

Oh, yes. In the <u>belly</u> of the beast.

Then what happened?

My banishment in Harar lasted three years, after which I was posted in the Ministry of the Interior under the close observation of the security machine. I finally managed to leave Ethiopia in 1972…

Given the Emperor's anger towards you, how did you manage to leave Ethiopia?

I have a child who was brain damaged at birth. By that time (she was born in 1966) she wasn't speaking and her movement was awkward. I couldn't find any medical facility or specialist. I applied to the World Bank in Washington, DC with a view towards getting the best specialist. It was almost a year before I could get permission from the Emperor. It is a long story. Getahun Tesema, the Minister of Interior, tried his best to mediate with Aklilu Habtewold, the prime minister. They knew the emperor was ill-disposed towards me so they told me I had to do it myself. They said, "If you can get anyone to take you to the emperor, then appeal directly." I was able to get someone to take me to the emperor. To make a long story short, having questioned me, he said OK.

At the World Bank, I worked as an attorney for a couple of years. The revolutionary upsurge in Ethiopia in Spring 1974 was to have an impact on my life as it did on many others. I had a certain reputation as a lawyer and human rights advocate, and it is that reputation, I believe, that led the members of the then-Ethiopian Parliament to elect me, in my absence, to serve as a member of the Commission of Inquiry appointed to investigate the wrong doings of Emperor Haile Selassie's government. Although I hesitated for a couple of months, I was finally persuaded by General Aman Andom, the first leader of the Dergue, to help in the investigation for a few months. I thus went back [to Ethiopia], without resigning my position at the World Bank, with the intention of helping out for some six months and returning to Washington. Things did not work out that way. Historic events occurred, producing their own logic and momentum. Instead of returning to Washington, I ended up in Eritrea.

Let's talk about your activities with the Commission of Inquiry. The so-called "Parliament of the Derg" was actually an Imperial Ethiopian Parliament from the Haile Selassie Era, right?

Yes, an imperial parliament. I wish to really clarify this because I have read some incorrect statements about it. That parliament was actually not the Derg's parliament. By that time, the parliament comprised of highly vocal and almost rebellious young people—mostly teachers. And some of them used to be my students. It was becoming increasingly restless. Because of my training and because of my attitude, I was appointed in absentia. We investigated the Wollo famine of 1973-74 for which we held the prime minister and his colleagues responsible for not responding in time. Under the existing penal code, their crime, criminal negligence, did not carry the death sentence. The maximum sentence we could impose was 15 years on all 40 or 50 of them. All we could do was submit our finding. Before the ink on our report was dry, they [the Derg] decided to massacre some 60 of the detainees including the ministers. They couldn't touch us because the commission inquiry was broadcast daily on the radio and we had gained some popularity. But they did kill them, including General Aman Andom [an Ethiopian of Eritrean ancestry and the first Ethiopian leader in post-Haile Selassie Ethiopia] because, they said, the commission was useless anyway.

Tell me about Aman Andom and why he was killed.

Because he was a very popular man, the emperor had kicked him upstairs—made him a senator. He was a senator for almost 10 years. When the young turks [the Derg soldiers] took over, they called upon him to come and lead them because most of them were non-commissioned officers and juniors. They were *asr aleka*, *amsa aleka* [junior officers] and so on.

So, they used the Commission's report as an excuse to kill people?

They were after blood. They wanted to massacre them for reasons known to themselves. They killed Aman because he didn't want a military solution to Eritrea and he refused to sign on to the execution plan. We were against it.

That's when you left Ethiopia for Eritrea?

I had to escape…Actually, I escaped in the nick of time. They were looking for me because I was a friend of Aman [Andom]. They were going to arrest anyone who had dealings with Aman. I got inside information and I escaped. A friend of mine, Desta Woldekidan, (in my novel, Riding the Whirlwind, I refer to him as Desta KidanWolde) took me by car to Mekele on a Saturday afternoon. He was connected to ELF fighters who were working in the city. He introduced me to one of them. It is a long story, but I reached Eritrea, after a hazardous journey, in late 1974 and first tried to join in the mass efforts mobilized to end the war between the ELF and the EPLF.

That was the civil war between ELF and EPLF where people from Asmara environs went to mediate?

The Weki Zagher meeting. October 1974. I arrived some six weeks afterwards. Jebha [ELF] attacked the EPLF at night after the Weki Zagher meeting. After we arrived, Mesfin Hagos [formerly Eritrea's Minister of Defense and, recently, a governor, and G-15] and others explained to me that the ELF only wanted a military solution as articulated in their first national congress—with Idris Adem as titular head and Herui [T. Bairou] as the man in charge. It was fresh in the memories of the people in the Karneshim area. Many of them knew the victims; women would weep. That was one of the saddest episodes in the history of the sad civil war.

When we finally convinced them to meet, in Ametsi—Herui, Isaias, Totil and others were there—that is when they agreed to stop the war and talk. That was the end of the hostilities. You can't imagine the jubilation of the public at the time.

We?

It wasn't a formal committee. It was a team of volunteer Eritreans. Two of us—myself and Radazghi Gebremedhin (Barba)- were seen as prominent but we were following up on the work of the village elders. We picked up the broken pieces, and many [civilians] volunteered as emissaries.

This actually answers my questions. Because one of my questions was: why did you choose EPLF over ELF? Unlike most Eritreans who joined a front either because they were conscripted or because they had a friend or relative in one of the fronts, or maybe one of the fronts was closest to their hometown, you actually had the luxury of choice. Was your choice based on the incidents of Weki Zagher?

That was one. But I had also observed, and I was a seasoned observer by then, I could tell differences in organization, in discipline, and quite frankly I saw the EPLF as better organized, better disciplined. I saw more openness, more tradition-bound discussion among members of the ELF. But judging from the situation as to which organization would take us to liberation, I made two and two and got four and said the EPLF is the better organization. This [EPLF] is the one that would lead the Eritrean people successfully to liberation.

Herui happened to be a good friend of mine. I knew him in England. I didn't know Isaias from Adam. Logically, from human relations standpoint, I would have gone to the ELF. Besides it was the ELF who brought me from Mekele to Eritrea.

Were you at all influenced by the reputation of the ELF as being "Ama Haradit" [ELF The Butcher]?

Not at all. I had observed in the highlands in Hazega, Adi Gebrai; I went back and forth several times. I saw many highly educated Asmarinos show camaraderie with the lowlanders. The ELF was like the EPLF: highland/lowland, Muslim/Christian. There was no difference in that respect. As for *"Ama Haradit"*, at that time, the height of the civil war, the story they [the ELF] were telling me about the EPLF was horrendous: *tSere gedli* [anti revolutionary], *medada*...

In my interview with Herui T. Bairou, I asked about "Sryet Addis" [ELF's alleged killing of new recruits from Addis Ababa.] Many former ELF fighters wrote me challenging that and blaming me for not asking Herui with specifics and names of victims. Do you know anything or anyone from "Sryet Addis"?

Not at all. It is a mystery to me. My answer to the "Who did what to whom" is always, "Let history and historians sort it out."

1975 – 1991

From 1975 – 1977, I was helping with the ERA and its work was relief, providing supplies, and food for children. After two years, given my background and training and given that my family was in Washington, DC, they agreed to let me go. They said, "You can help us more there."

From 1977 – 1985, I was doing odd jobs: lecturing, traveling, writing and occasionally being tasked to approach people in the State Department. It became a diplomatic work-at-large without specific appointment.

In 1985, the leadership appointed me as a representative to the UN; between 1985-1991, without observer status. I used to call it "Mission Impossible." Many of the big governments wouldn't touch us with a 10 foot pole. Some of the Scandinavian countries took pity on us. As the war progressed and the chances of Eritrean victory increased, people would seek us out and ask questions. We would show them videotapes of the bombing of Massawa. That shocked most of them—and we made copies to send to their ministries.

After independence, wouldn't you have been the logical choice to be Eritrea's ambassador to the United States or American Ambassador to Eritrea?

Many people say that. I wouldn't have wanted to. My energies from 1991 onwards were focused on being with my family and on rebuilding my income. My income had stagnated; I sometimes had to borrow money to support my family. I didn't expect it [an appointment] and I wouldn't have accepted it. I have no ambition whatsoever in that regards: that's what I want to make clear to your readers. As a matter of fact, at heart, I am a professional with poetic bent; I hate politics. You just join the fray when the fate of your country is at risk. Seeking public office, etc, no thank you. I am very happy in my professional life. Why would I leave a comfortable life for the misery of being somebody's underling? Or even being a leader? But how do you convince people of that? I guess they are entitled to their opinion.

THE DRAFTING OF THE CONSTITUTION

The following questions will deal with trying to address a common criticism: that the Eritrean constitution was not the work of an independent body. Allegedly, the EPLF, somewhere in Nakfa, had written the constitution and all the commission did, or was asked

to do, was put on some makeup on it to legitimize it. So, let's begin at the beginning. In law, there is a principle that you lawyers have: don't ask a question unless you already know the answer. Why do you think Isaias contacted you and not some other lawyers to head up the constitution drafting process?

Isaias did not know what kind of constitution I would come up. I have been told that President Isaias actually asked someone else—another lawyer—and that lawyer declined. And the reason he declined was by saying, "here you have someone who was with you and someone who happens to be a constitutional lawyer: he teaches it, he breathes it. Why wouldn't you ask him?" It was after the man declined, that I was approached.

You were not approached because the president must have felt you have too much of an independent streak?

Absolutely. I never had really a cushy comfy relationship with Isaias. There was mutual respect. I respected him for his brilliant mind, an organizing mind. And, I suppose, he respected my credentials. I was too much of a maverick to do what he wanted me to do. There is another point: I wrote, "The Future Political System of Eritrea" (1989-90) and, when he read it, I am told he hit the roof. The EPLF was already in Afabet [1988]: they were waiting. I am sure they were entertaining ideas about the constitution of an independent Eritrea. In the pamphlet, I spell out the central principles of a constitution. In it, I sketched the central ideas that should go into the making of a constitutional democracy, including the rule of law, separation of powers, judicial independence, and pluralist politics. Above all, I speculated, in fact I expected, that multi-parties should be allowed after independence, in accordance with the 2nd [EPLF] Congress, which I attended. I wasn't really writing anything new, antagonist or original. I was simply extrapolating. This is obviously speculation, but I assume that the reason why Isaias showed displeasure at my booklet was that, with the reputation I had, I could influence too many people.

Were the merits and the adoption of multi-party democracy in Eritrea discussed in the 2ⁿᵈ Congress or was it just placed there as a decorative piece?

It was debated, discussed. The cadres, the middle cadres of the EPLF, had by then abandoned the Marxist dogma. They had read the disasters of one-party states of Africa. Isaias, being a politician, wouldn't want to go against the grain. In my view, he probably thought he would cross that bridge when he gets to it.

When we started drafting the constitution, within a year of the constitution making process, the PFDJ came up with a document widely circulated talking about *Guided Democracy*. We got a copy. The question that faced us was whether the PFDJ was prepared for multi-parties. I remember telling some of my colleagues that unless they [the PFDJ] categorically declared that they are in favor of multi-parties, I would have to rethink my position in terms of continuing to serve as Chair of the Commission. We met with the executive body of the PFDJ: Isaias was present. I asked the question point blank. I said, "are you willing to allow multi-party system in Eritrea; yes or no." They looked at each other. Isaias said something to the effect "this is not subject to debate. It was resolved in the 2ⁿᵈ Congress. I came to this meeting to discuss problems of logistics and if there are things in which we can be of help, etc. I got work to do." And left. Later on, the others answered my question in the affirmative. The issue of multi-parties was discussed in all public discussions

We are getting a little ahead of ourselves. Let's go to when was the first time the "offer" to draft the Eritrean constitution brought to your attention? By whom? Was this discussed in pre-liberation of Eritrea?

Early in the summer of 1993, a telex message came from Asmara sent by President Isaias asking if I would be able to head a constitution drafting entity. I was willing and excited to do it, but I was not sure whether I would be able to accept at the time. I had long been involved in the Eritrean struggle, as I explained already. As EPLF representative at the United

Nations, I had to travel a lot, which had made my family life difficult and negatively affected my income earning capacity. In July 1993 during my visit to Asmara, Isaias formally asked me whether I was ready to take up the post of Chairman of the Eritrean Constitutional Commission. I accepted with one condition. I asked him to write a letter to the President of Howard University where I had been teaching for the previous sixteen years. He agreed and did write the letter, which I hand-carried and delivered, but Howard University was not willing to accommodate me in terms of giving me suitable leave of absence. It was for that reason that I left Howard for North Carolina—a lily white university—which was not only willing to give me the needed leave but created an endowed Chair for me and hired me at much higher salary! But that's another story.

I never discussed the idea of writing a constitution before liberation.

Who tasked you and the group that eventually became the Constitutional Commission of Eritrea (CCE)?

The formal appointment of the Commission was made by the Transitional National Assembly.

And who was in the Transitional National Assembly?

They are the Central Committee members of EPLF. This was before their third congress so it was still the EPLF.

The eyebrow-raisers are going to say that the Central Committee and the Constitutional Commission was all EPLF. 100%.

That is in the nature of things and should not surprise us. The announcement of the appointment of the Commission came out early in 1994, with the list of the majority of their names. As to who actually selected the members to be presented to the National Assembly, you know or should know that there is only one source for all appointments. Members of the inner circle of the governing Front play a crucial role in suggesting names for appointment, and they in turn may consult others among their close friends and associates for suggestions. But ultimately, the President has the final say, and the National Assembly has tended to accept whatever the President proposes.

But in one particular respect at least, the President accepted much of what I asked. Let me backtrack a bit and say that he had asked me to draft the law that established the Commission, which became Proclamation N. 55. I drafted the law in the Fall of 1993 and it came out early in 1994. Meanwhile, I met Isaias during one of his visits to the United States. I gave him a list of names of people, mostly lawyers, who I thought should be members of the Executive Committee of the Commission. With the exception of two names, he accepted my request.

How many members did the commission have? Who are they? Their background?

The commission members were supposedly 50; but the list had about 47. Ten members made up the Executive Committee and the rest formed the General Council. All were nominated by the National Assembly including the Chairman, Vice Chairman and the Secretary.

Let me start with the members of the Executive Committee, which was the central organ of the Commission and conducted meetings on a weekly basis. I was the Chairman, Azien Yassin [formerly with the ELF Executive Committee] was the Vice Chairman and Zemehret Yohannes [PFDJ Cultural Affairs] was the Secretary of the Commission. The other seven were: Dr. Amare Tekle, [who oversaw the referendum process]; Mr. Idris Gelawdios, [one of the founders of the ELF, then living in Cairo, lawyer by training, deceased]; Dr. Seyoum Haregot, (then with the UNDP); Ms. Amna Naib, (Eritrean Ministry of Justice); Ms. Zahra Jaber, (now mayor of Keren); Mr. Paulos Tesfagiorgis (a lecturer of law at Asmara University); and Mr. Musa Naib, who studied law in Addis Ababa in 1970s [formerly Mayor of Massawa, and is now Advocate General.]

The names of the members of the Council were made public at the time. It included people who had been with PLF, like Mr. Taha Mohamed Nur [Foreign Office]; it included Jafer Abubaker (Ph.D. in Public Administration) who died about 3 years ago.

What was the criteria used to select them? What was the background of the group during the liberation struggle and post independence?

I have no direct knowledge of the process of the selection of the members of the Commission, except in the case of some of the members of the Executive Committee, as I already explained. But informal talks that I had with some members of the National Assembly indicated to me that the primary consideration in selecting the members of the Commission was their participation in Eritrea's liberation struggle. Indeed, the vast majority of the members were liberation fighters. The few cases of members who were not liberation fighters reflected the concern of the appointing authorities for representation in terms of ethnic, religious and gender balance. There is, of course, an important condition – they must not have worked with the enemy working against Eritrea during the struggle.

If you examine the list of the members of the Commission, you will find that the factors of balance were satisfied, more or less. All the nine ethnic groups of Eritrea were represented. The two major religions, Christianity and Islam, were represented on equal basis. And there were 23 women members, which represented 47% of the total membership.

In terms of age, the average age of the members of the Commission was about fifty. The youngest member was a thirty-two year old former fighter while the oldest member was an eighty-year-old former judge of the high court who unfortunately died during the second year of the constitution-making process.

Incidentally, two members of the Executive Committee—Azien Yassin and Idris Gelawdios—also died before the end of the process, both of kidney failure. Their loss was keenly felt by the Commission and by me specially, not least because they died young and had so much contribution to make to their nation. Azien's kidney had failed before the start of the work of the Commission. I wish to take this opportunity to pay homage to brothers Azien and Idris. Azien's presence during the inauguration of the work of the Commission in March 1994 and thereafter, despite his serious illness, was a source of great joy and inspiration to the rest of us. He had to leave for Saudi Arabia because there was no kidney dialysis facility in Asmara, but we kept in touch through the telephone and fax messages. As I valued his contribution, I consulted with him on a number of critical issues.

Azien was a dedicated and universally respected man among his fellow freedom fighters, and a man of great charm and intellect. I liked him as I also like Idris who was equally dedicated and respected among his former fellow fighters. I chose Idris to chair the Economic Committee of the Commission which he discharged with diligence, with Dr. Yemane Misghinna acting as his assistant and secretary of the sub-committee.

As for the question as to the members' role in the post-independence situation, the former fighters were all involved in the work of the government in various capacities. The others were engaged in their respective trades or professions. For instance, there was a member representing the private/commercial sector in his capacity as the President of the Chamber of Commerce. In terms of social and professional background, many members had background in teaching or teacher education. Not less than ten had legal education or were involved in legal practice in some form at some time in their careers. The majority of the ten members of the Executive Committee had legal education.

You have made a good case that the commission was well represented in terms of gender, region, ethnicity, profession, age etc. How about ideologically: left, center left? Was this not a big deal?

Yes. It was a big deal. The whole question of left, right, center politics is really peripheral to the Eritrean life to the extent that the Marxist point of view espoused by which the EPLF's actions and programs were colored was important during the struggle. It was a point of contention between ELF and EPLF as to who is redder. Even then, it was superficial. But someone had to find a reason to distinguish himself: in the 1960s, 1970s this was the criteria of acceptance in the world. It was logical at the time to want to prove you were more left than the other. With the collapse of the Soviet Union, it became a moot issue. What was important is whether the government considered you loyal enough not to upset the scheme.

The issue was not who appointed us but whether we were (a) autonomous or (b) whether we did our job satisfactorily. Did we involve the public? What was the quality of the documents we distributed? And how did we utilize it? How about the quality of the constitution itself?

To those who say, "they are all EPLF people" my rhetoric answer is "every government—even military governments—have a right and have appointed their own committees to develop constitutions that work." It doesn't mean members of the entity shouldn't consider different interests. If we are to examine lack of representation: why didn't the EPLF allow the ELF to come in as an organization? That was the sin I committed in 1990 when I wrote the booklet: I suggested the ELF should be allowed to compete. If that had happened the ELF would have insisted on representation. Given the fact that the EPLF was a one-party government, I wouldn't expect such kind of representation. Is the entity representative enough in terms of religion, gender? Are the members considered wise and have integrity to raise questions. The answer is yes. People like Azien Yassin would have challenged us: it is a pity that he died so early.

Part II

As a constitutional scholar, what do you think of Eritrea's first constitution? Was it "Anze Matienzo's constitution" or was it the result of consultations with all the constituencies concerned?

To start with, we need to be clear about one thing. The constitution you are referring to—the 1952 Constitution—was not the constitution of an independent country; it was one imposed on Eritrea by the United Nations, based on the famous (infamous to Eritreans) UN General Assembly Resolution (390A) which joined Eritrea with Ethiopia in a lopsided federal arrangement. Under that arrangement, Eritrea had no sovereignty, but was a federated unit with Ethiopia "under the sovereignty of the Ethiopian Crown," to use the phrase of the Resolution. I call it lopsided because Eritrea as the federating unit was a junior partner, subordinate to Ethiopia as the dominant partner.

There is a sense in which it can be called Anze Matienzo's constitution in that he had control over the process of its making. If there was any consultation, the most significant was the one he had with Ethiopian Prime Minister Aklilu Habtewold and Emperor Haile Selassie whose views he eagerly sought and accommodated. Following the adoption of UN Resolution 390A, the Eritrean political forces that had been demanding for independence were disheartened. Although some attempts were made by some of them to minimize imperial encroachment on the internal affairs and to maximize Eritrea's autonomy under the imposed constitution, in the end the cards were stacked against them.

Nonetheless, despite its defects, the 1952 Constitution had several positive aspects, including a Bill of Rights, and Article 16 which provided that the Constitution was based on fundamental principles of democracy. The panel of experts who met in Geneva to draft it faced the challenge of writing a democratic Constitution for a unit that was to be joined with a feudal system, as Sir Ivor Jennings (one of the draftsmen) has recorded in his book "Approach to Independence." Indeed, Emperor Haile Selassie was forced to promulgate the Revised Constitution of Ethiopia in 1955, as a consequence of that challenge. (See my article, "Constitutional Development in Ethiopia", Journal of African Studies, 1966.)

Between the conclusion of the first draft of the constitution presented by the Constitutional Commission of Eritrea (CCE) and the ratification of the document three years later by the National Assembly, there were many public seminars and sessions held. What was changed in the constitution as a result of these seminars and the feedback of the people?

First a word on the context—an explanation of what we call process-driven constitution making. Two basic objectives are implied in process-driven constitution making: the first, and most important objective is constructive engagement of the largest majority of the population. This is necessary in order to ensure that the end product of the process—the constitution—is seen as legitimate, and owned by the people. It is critical that the people have a sense of ownership of the basic document by which they are governed, and this can only be achieved through their direct participation in the making of the constitution. The second objective is to tap on the native genius and experience of the population.

The Eritrean constitution making experience, starting from the content of the law establishing the Commission to the strategy and organization of the work of the Commission, reflected this objective.

Was the purpose achieved? In terms of the widest possible participation of the public, and their sense of ownership of the product of the process, the answer is definitely yes. And how was it achieved? The Commission distributed education material, including several international legal instruments such as the Universal Declaration of Human Rights, and wrote appropriate booklets suitable for Eritrea's condition, in several Eritrean languages and broadcast them on the radio. This was designed to enable members of the public to make optimum contribution in raising their awareness and thus raise questions and giving opinions. Such questions and opinions were recorded in public meetings, collated and analyzed by the Commission and are part of the public record. The first phase of the process included an intense civic education campaign that used these materials.

When finally, we sat down to draft the constitution and to discuss the draft, the views of the public were taken into account. I can cite some examples at the appropriate time when we discuss some of the Articles; but let me give one example to illustrate the dynamics of the process of give and take between the Commission and the Eritrean public. This concerns the words of the oath of office of the President, and of the members of the National Assembly and judges. In our original draft, the oath was to be sworn in the name of our martyrs, with no mention of Allah or God. When the draft was submitted for public debate in the Summer and Autumn of 1996, there was widespread complaint raising objection to the absence of the Creator. You see, we had been carried away with our concern to establish a secular State and our desire to make our martyrs the center of such a secular ethos, forgetting that ours is a deeply religious society. In the end, we took this public objection into account and changed the oath.

The Preamble

The last paragraph of the preamble to the Constitution says, "today…, on this historic date…solemnly ratify officially…this Constitution." Why wasn't an implementation date included?

Why indeed! We live and learn, as they say. When we consider this question in retrospect, with the hindsight of nearly four years after the ratification of the constitution, we must admit that it was a mistake not to fix an effective date, or at least specify a maximum period after which the Constitution would come into full force and effect. We have been justly criticized for this omission, but it was not an oversight or lack of foresight on our part. As I have had occasion to explain in a previous posting in the Internet, we left it open deliberately in order to give the government a chance to clear the deck—to change or abolish laws that were in violation of the Constitution. The notorious example of such law is the so-called ant-corruption law. It was an act or omission based on trust—a belief that the government would clear the deck and implement the Constitution. I had expected this to be done before the end of 1997, or at the latest, by the Spring of 1998, by which time I expected serious preparations to be under way for elections to the National Assembly and the office of the President in accordance with the Constitution.

I will not repeat here why I think the government postponed the implementation of the constitution; I have covered it in a previous posting causing a raging controversy. Suffice it to say now that the government seems to be responding to public pressure to implement the constitution. We'll see. We shall see what we shall see, as Mr. Pickwick said, or was it Mr. Mcauber?

Article 1 (1) What does it mean to base a State on the principles of "social justice?' What is "social justice?" Does it have the same meaning as defined by PFDJ in its Charter? (2) Why weren't the territories of Eritrea described in further detail? (3) Why did CCE settle on having a "unitary government"?

(1) First let me explain the meaning of the concept of social justice and its place in the constitutional scheme of things. And this will actually answer the first part of the question that asks what a State based on social justice means. Second, we need to be aware of the fact that social justice is a universal principle and its articulation in the PFDJ Charter does not represent the discovery of a new principle by the men who wrote the Charter. Social justice is part of the common heritage of humankind, as are democracy and the rule of law. Article 1(1) of the constitution says that Eritrea is founded on "the principles of democracy, social justice and the rule of law." This is a general statement of principles and, as such, is necessarily concise. Its detailed articulation (definition) and application is left to another article of the Constitution and to future legislation to be enacted by the National Assembly. Article 21 of the Constitution (Economic, Social and Cultural Rights and Responsibilities) provides that "every citizen shall have equal access to publicly funded social services," and that the State "shall endeavor, within the limit of its resources, to make available to all citizens health, education, cultural and other social services."

One additional point. The philosophical or ideological underpinning of social justice is the general belief that justice is indivisible: that the basic social services like education, health, affordable housing should not be reserved to those who have the means. For if access to such vital services (as well as access to food resources) is allowed to some and not to others, there would be no social peace. This belief is as old as there have been good people on this good earth, but its application as a universal principle is of recent origin and its general acceptance is the result of slow social progress. Under such general belief, the State is required to secure, within its available means, the social welfare of all citizens particularly those who are disadvantaged. The old belief: "everyone for himself and the devil take the hindmost" is no longer acceptable.

(2). As to the question why the territories of Eritrea were not described in more detail, my first reaction is to answer it with another question: "why should they be described in detail?" The constitution says: "The territory of Eritrea consists of all its territories, including the islands, territorial waters and airspace delineated by recognized boundaries." Getting into more details than this would mean counting the number of islands, naming zobas (regions) and districts etc., which is not only not necessary in a constitution, but would raise unnecessary problems. The problem of attempting to be exhaustive or all-inclusive in legal drafting is that you may end up leaving something out. So, you resort to the generic concept which encompasses everything under the category you are dealing with. I generally use the fancy name and call this Legal Drafting 101!

Let me also use this question to make a point about our decision to settle for a concise constitution, rather than a long one. When drafting a Constitution, constitution makers are faced with two principal questions: a) what should be included in a constitution, and b) how long should it be? These questions raise another question: How does one determine what should, or should not, be included in a constitution? The Constitutional Commission of Eritrea answered the last question by drawing up a list of questions immediately after its inaugural meeting in March, 1994, and submitting them for public debate. Following the civic education phase (late 1994-early 1995), the Commission drew up a list of Proposals embracing the principal constitutional issues, and submitted them for public discussion, in mid 1995. One of the points raised in the Proposals concerned the nature and scope of the constitution. The Commission decided on a concise constitution, rather than on a long one, and explained why the constitution had to be concise, and why it had to be written in a general way rather than in detail, leaving its detailed implementation to legislation.

This conclusion and the adoption of a concise constitution were based on a thorough debate on the merits and demerits of different models—concise versus long. The controlling criteria was: the current needs of the country, its historical condition, its culture and social structure. Concerning this issue, the consensus among constitutional scholars is that a good constitution is one that is concise, that has a *"judicious mixture of definiteness in principle with elasticity in detail"*, as the noted British scholar and jurist, Lord Brice, put it in extolling the American constitution—its brevity, and the simplicity of its language.

3. As to why we settled on having a unitary government, the Commission did research and debated the question whether Eritrea needed a federal or unitary system. The answer to this question depends on a number of factors, principal among them being the size of the country, its resource endowments and their distribution, the history of it national unity, and its ethnic make-up. Countries like Nigeria or Ethiopia with their large size, complex ethnic make-up and histories of conflict have chosen a federal structure. The Commission considered that Eritrea, with its smaller size, history of national struggle and relatively united ethnic groups, does not need a federal structure. Instead, it should have a unitary system with its component regions enjoying appropriate degrees of autonomy to be determined by legislation. In determining the degree of autonomy, such legislation would take into account: the resource endowments of the regions and their general development in administrative capacity and financial resources. The present division of the administrative regions of Eritrea seems to have been motivated by similar considerations; but is a subject that may need to be reviewed from time to time.

Article 2(sub. 2) If the constitution was ratified on May 24, 1997, does it mean that many of the laws passed that are not based on the constitution are "null and void?" (sub. 5) Is the lack of transparency in the "conduct of the affairs of the government and all organizations and institutions" unconstitutional?

I would answer question (2) in a larger context, in addition to the fate of existing laws that are not based on the constitution. First of all, some of these laws are in violation of the constitution and would be null and void once the constitution comes into effect. Second, most laws, not being in violation of the constitution, would continue to apply unless and until they are revised or abolished by an Act of Parliament (the National Assembly).

So, when does a constitution come into effect? The question of whether a constitution comes into effect upon its ratification has been raised by Eritreans, who were frustrated by the government's inordinate delay in implementing it. Some Eritrean lawyers have argued that it should be considered as having come into effect the minute it was ratified, even in the absence of a provision specifying an effective date. It is a compelling view on the face of it, one that some of us have been tempted to want to support. The opposite view would raise the obvious question: then why have we been complaining about the government's delay in implementing the constitution? I would divide the subject into two from the perspective of the application of the constitution. The first concerns the establishment of institutions in accordance with the requirements of the constitution, notably the National Assembly which has to be elected. This, in our case, has to await the promulgation of an electoral law and related legislation that would provide the necessary legal framework for the formation of a constitutionally based government. This long-overdue legislation will hopefully be in place, and whether we agree or disagree with the outcome of the election that is supposed to take place at the end of the year, it is a step in the right direction.

The second area concerns the Bill of Rights provision of the Constitution—the whole of Chapter three. It is my considered opinion and that of many others that this part of the constitution should be presumed to have come into effect upon the ratification of the constitution and should be applied. Accordingly, the so-called anti-corruption law should be regarded as unconstitutional. This conclusion has serious implication in terms of the accountability of the authorities responsible for ignoring the Bill of Rights provisions of the constitution by continuing to apply laws that are in violation of those provisions.

Who will make determination on such issues of accountability and the question of whether the Bill of Rights provision of the constitution is presumed to apply upon the ratification of the constitution? Who else? The Supreme Court, of course.

Does lack of transparency constitute violation of the constitution, in view of the requirements of Article 2(5)?

In order to answer this question fairly, we need to reproduce the whole of the sub-article 5. It provides:

"Pursuant to the provisions of this constitution and other laws, the conduct of the affairs of government and all organizations and institutions shall be accountable and transparent."

This is a difficult question to answer in hypothetical terms; we have to cite concrete cases of lack of transparency and also define the type of conduct in relation to which a person may be accused of acting in violation of the constitution. There are degrees of transparency and of accountability depending on the nature of the "affairs of government and all organizations and institutions." Note also the wording of sub-article 5: it says, "pursuant to this constitution and other laws." In other words, any complainant accusing any official of lack of transparency will have to relate the accusation to the law, citing specific articles of the constitution or other law, which requires such transparency. In the case of a government official, for instance, if a public hearing is contemplated by a piece of legislation from which such official derives his authority and interested parties have a right to an open hearing but are not give such open hearing, the official would be answerable for his failure. The remedy for the aggrieved party may be administrative, judicial, or political. Administrative redress may be requested pursuant to article 24 of the constitution. The complainant may also seek judicial redress; he may bring an action in an ordinary court of law. Alternatively, the recourse may be political; the aggrieved party may complain to his Member of Parliament elected from his constituency and seek redress by having the responsible minister to answer in a parliamentary hearing. I am assuming we will have an elected National Assembly. I am also assuming that we shall have progressed from the domain of personal rule to the reign of the Rule of Law!

PART III

[Article 3] **How does one define "Eritrean father or mother"?**

According to Article 3(1) of the constitution, "any person born of an Eritrean father or mother is an Eritrean citizen." Note the word "or." In terms of this constitutional provision, it is not only a child who is the issue of a union between two Eritrean citizens that can be a citizen. The point of interest in this respect, and one that was the subject of questions and comments during the constitution making process, is that the parents do not have to be both citizens in order for their child to claim Eritrean citizenship; a child can claim citizenship on his mother as well as on his father's side.

Many disputed the position of the Commission that citizenship can be claimed on the mother's side. This position, which is contrary to the traditional thinking of Eritrean society, is one of the revolutionary principles espoused by the EPLF during the liberation struggle. It is based on the equality principle between men and women—one of the articles of faith of the revolution. Some asked point blank: "What if the father is an Ethiopian or a Yemeni, and the son eventually runs for the office of the president of Eritrea? Wouldn't this pose a security risk?" The answer was that there will be no compromise on the principle of equality between men and women, and that the electorate should be trusted to determine whether any candidate would, or would not, be a security risk. We have to cross that bridge when we reach it.

I guess I should have been clearer with my question. My question is what makes the father or the mother Eritrean? How far back does the ancestry have to go before one claims citizenship? Was the citizenship proclamation advanced for the purposes of the Referendum implicitly accepted?

The Law on citizenship was issued with the referendum in mind. The issue of citizenship is linked with the question when Eritrea became a nation recognized under international law. Eritrea's origin as a nation-state is Italian colonial rule, which started in January 1890. Between then and the takeover of the British, the inhabitants were Italian colonial subjects. (NB: subjects, not citizens with full civil and political rights.) Any inhabitant of Italian Eritrea who needed to travel before 1941, had to have documents issued by Italian authorities. (It would be interesting to research under what kind of document and status Zerai Deress travelled from Asmara to Rome in the 1930s.) The Proclamation of citizenship that the Eritrean government issued before the 1993 referendum uses a cut-off date for claiming citizenship–1937, if my memory serves me right, because to insist on going back to the beginning of Eritrea's origin as a new nation-state would have been not only unrealistic but unjust to a whole community of people who were born and brought up in Eritrea thinking of themselves and acting as Eritreans. Anyone interested in the detailed provision of the law has to look it up.

Art.4(1) The Eritrean flag is described in such detail, what is left to be determined by law? Was there ever a discussion of this or was this deference shown to EPLF/PFDJ? Did members of the CCE (the Commission) who had ELF or PLF background question this? Art. 4(3) What does "the equality of all Eritrean languages is guaranteed" mean? Was there consideration given to having official languages? Was this subject discussed at length?

(1) With respect to the flag, two things are left to be determined by legislation:1) the dimension, and 2) a description of what the various colors represent symbolically. However, the point of your question is well taken. The issue of the flag did not occasion any debate during the constitution making process. What was retained without any discussion of any significance was what the EPLF adopted at its third Congress. Before that Congress, the Provisional government had adopted the same flag with the same description, with additional specifications on the dimension. [See Proclamation 37/1993 issued to define the powers and functions of the government. Article 10 of that law specifies the dimension as 105 x 210 centimeters.]

This is an issue on which due deference was given to the existing flag, pre-determined by the EPLF, being the Front that attained Eritrean independence. In my recollection, none of the members of CCE who had ELF or PLF background raised any objections on the flag issue at the meetings of the Commission.

(3) Concerning language, it must to be said that this was one of the most controversial issues throughout the process. The debate on the language question may be grouped into four axes of division. a) The people who insisted that Arabic and Tigrigna should be declared official languages. b) Those who argued that Arabic, Tgrigna and Tigre should be made official languages. c) Those who argued that Tigrigna and Tigre should be official languages, being languages of over eighty percent of the Eritrean population. d) And then there was the Commission's position, which was what was accepted and ratified.

The case for having a national language or languages (on the bases of a, b or c) was argued on the ground that a nation needs a language for common communication as an essential condition for nation building. The adopted solution—simply declaring the equality of languages—was grounded on the principle of the equality of all ethnic groups and on the consequent need (and right) of every citizen to use the language of his/her choice for educational and other purposes. The majority of Eritreans that participated in the process were persuaded by this argument, and the Commission felt justified in writing the essence of the argument into the constitution. However, the continued use of Arabic and Tigrigna as working languages, with its origin in the armed struggle, was duly noted, and it was left to the future to determine if there is a need for official language(s).

I have a few questions on the subject of official languages:

(a) Doesn't the status of Arabic and Tigrigna as official languages pre-date the armed struggle? If you recall, my question on the 1952 Constitution [Part II of the interview] was trying to discern to what degree it reflected the wishes of the Eritrean people. There is

sufficient historical evidence, isn't there, that on the issue of selecting official languages, the choice of Tigrigna/Arabic reflected the wishes of the overwhelming majority of Eritreans. Certainly, the choice of Arabic reflected the wishes of Eritrean Muslims. What evidence was presented to the CCE that the wish of the people had altered so radically that they no longer wished Tigirigna/Arabic as official languages?

(b) In the second congress of the ELF, when the front chose to implement Arabic/Tigrigna as official languages, the strongest proponents of defeating the proposition that Tigre be a co-official language were Tigre-speakers themselves. Given this, is it not reasonable to assume that the Tigirigna/Tigre proposal is advocated by "anything-but-Arabic" proponents?

(c) Given that Arabic/Tigrigna was the choice of Eritrea during the Federation Era, given that Arabic/Tigrigna was the choice of a segment of Eritrea during the height of the ELF, isn't the denial of Arabic/Tigrigna as official languages simply a manifestation of EPLF/PFDJ wishes that was adopted by the CCE?

(d) Wasn't this issue so divisive that a key figure in the CCE, Taha Mohammed Nur [who, like his brother Haji Musa Mohammed Nur died in jail], resigned in protest?

(e) What is the difference between "working" language and "official" language?

The answer to

(a) is that yes, Arabic and Tigrigna were official languages under the 1952 constitution, and it did reflect the wishes of the Eritrean people as represented by their different political parties or groups. There was no public debate on it or on any other issue, as I said in my previous answer. But it was generally accepted as a sound policy, given the need to create unity among the principal political actors of the time.

As to the question what evidence was produced to the CCE that the wishes of the people was altered., I repeat that there is no evidence to prove that the majority of the people wanted Arabic/and Tigrigna to be official languages. What CCE did was to begin with the first principle nurtured during the armed struggle of the equality of languages. The convergence of CCE's approach and the official position of the EPLF on this issue may lead some to believe that this was dictated by the EPLF. It was not. CCE consulted with EPLF leaders, of course and the view on the principle of the equality of languages as the determining factor was strongly argued by members of the top leadership of the EPLF/PFDJ. [Incidentally, this answers the question in (c)]

The story of Tigre speakers insisting on the inclusion of their language as co-equal with Arabic and Tigrigna at the 2nd congress of the ELF, if true, is heartening: more power to them. The question is why didn't the other (minority) groups make a similar demand? Perhaps because they did not have a strong representation at the congress or their leaders at the time felt that Arabic and Tigrigna would serve their interests. I think to say that our decision was based on the sentiment of "anything but Arabic" has not basis on fact and, although there may be people in the PFDJ who entertain such a sentiment, it can't be the reflection of the majority.

(c) See above

(d) It is not true that Taha resigned in protest, as you say. Taha was one of the few members of CCE who strongly argued in favor of Arabic being one of the official languages, but he stayed as a member right to the end.

[Chapter II]
Article 6(1) What does "unity-in-diversity" mean?

National unity and stability is a basic condition for a peaceful life and for optimum development. At the same time, there must be recognition of the need of the component parts of the nation to maintain their identity. The concept of unity-in-diversity encapsulates the goal of mediating between the need for unity while guaranteeing diversity—tolerance of diversity of views and cultures and of the existence and growth of different groups within a political community embraced within a nation.

[Article 7(2)]: What does "human rights of women" mean? Is human rights a concept that has universal definition?

Again, it is necessary to reproduce the whole of Article 7(2)—"Any act that violates the human rights of women or limits or otherwise thwarts their role and participation is prohibited." During the long public discourse on the constitution and the Proposal that presaged it, the question of how best to put the equality of women with men in constitutional terms was one of the most hotly debated issues. Some wanted a detailed provision, while others thought that singling out the women issues would demean them and raise another question, which is contained in the second part of your question, i.e., the universality of human rights. Some people raised the question: If human rights is a universal concept—and it is—then why provide for it separately for women? [See Article 14(1) of the constitution which ordains that "All persons are equal under the law." See also Sub-Article 2 of the same Article, which prohibits discrimination on the basis of gender...etc.]

In deciding to include Article 7(2), providing for the special protection of women, the Commission considered the Eritrean condition in which women have historically taken a subordinate position and have, in innumerable instances, suffered humiliation. The revolution fought to change all that, but the struggle continues; traditions die hard. Hence the need for an express provision to send a clear signal to society.

Do human rights have a universal definition? Yes, it does, particularly since 1948, the year when the Universal Declaration of Human Rights was proclaimed. To Eritreans, much as we honor and respect the international legal instruments on human rights, the source of our human rights as citizens of the Eritrea nation is not only the important international conventions, but rather "the vital humanity," as an Eritrean writer has put it. [*Samuel Gebre-Adionai, paying tribute to his fallen comrades wrote; I have seen men and women pitted against steel, as if they were made of steel, and winning. I salute my martyred comrades in my remembrance of their vital humanity which stood up to fight, unbending to the will of the enemy, until the last drop of their blood—the precious blood which was the source of their being."*]

On Article 7.2, the definition of Human Rights for women, there is some discrepancy between how a State defines equity and how religion, for example a traditional practice of Islam, treats equity, particularly in civil law. How does the constitution reconcile the right to practice religion with the Rights of women?

I see no conflict between the right to practice religion and the rights of women. If you mean the possible conflict between the constitutionally guaranteed rights of women and some aspects of the Sharia under which women do not enjoy a full measure of rights such as equal division of property in the event of divorce, and custodial rights, then my answer is that women have an option to sue in the civil courts, and risk ostracism from their Muslim communities. But the equality principle applies to them and where there are clashes between the constitutional rights with those of the Sharia and tradition, it is up to the individual woman to make the choice. This will involve social action, as well as, or more than legal remedies.

[Article 10(2)]: What is "quick and equitable judgements" within the context of Eritrean tradition?

In a competent judicial system, the courts are required to conduct speedy trials and hand down equitable judgements. As the saying goes, delayed (or expensive) justice is no justice. There have been widespread public complaints that the courts do not render quick justice. The reasons are many, but the main reason is the shortage of appropriately trained judges and other judicial personnel. It will take many years before the constitutional requirement of quick justice is fulfilled.

[Article 8] (Sub.1) Is "social justice" a responsibility of the State? (Sub.3) Does regulation of land mean, by definition, ownership of land?

I have answered Q. 1 in Part I of the Interview

(Sub. 3) Regulation of land does not necessarily mean ownership. The regulatory power of the State—any State—is different from its ownership of any assets. Ownership of land has been a controversial issue. In Eritrea's case its resolution is crystallized in Article 23.

[Article 9(1)] How does a State enrich culture? And why does the State have responsibility for this?

The relevant section of the constitution provides:

"The State shall be responsible for creating and promoting conditions conducive for developing a national culture capable of expressing national identity, unity and progress of the Eritrean people." [Article 9(1)]

National culture should be distinguished from local (ethnic-based) cultures although there is a sense in which the two may be linked in that national culture can have roots in some of the dominant local cultures or may be influenced by them in its development. The national culture, in turn, can have a powerful impact through the Media and the educational system. The role played by modern Medial and the educational system imposes a regulatory function on the State. Its command of resources also adds a responsibility to the State to help in the sustenance and development of local cultures, through the provision of financial and logistical support. Such role indirectly facilitates the development of a sense of national unity-in-diversity.

Chapter III [Article 14(2)] The clause against discrimination forbids discrimination against many protected groups and then states "or any other improper factors." What are other factors?

This additional phrase is designed to preclude any derogation or limitation from the generality of the equality provision, which ordains that all persons are equal under the law. It is a kind of insurance against the possibility of omission, omission of any factor not enumerated in the Article.

Even the United States enumerates what classes are protected by law; anything that is not included in the Civil Rights Act, is not protected. The Eritrean constitution takes a more expansive list and leaves it up to future legislators and jurists to define what is "proper" or "improper" discrimination. Is this prudent?

Yes, it is. In this respect we are better than the Americans, a point worth celebrating!

[Article 15(1)]: Implicit in the provision "No person shall be deprived of life without due process of law" is the permission of capital punishment. Why?

Your assumption is correct; capital punishment is permitted under the Eritrean constitution, as it is under the American and many other constitutions. Under these constitutions, a person may be subject to the death penalty upon commission of a crime for which the death penalty is prescribed as the punishment. Under the present penal code of Eritrea, for example, a person may be punished by death for murder and treason under aggravated circumstances.

Capital punishment has been a subject of controversy in recent years. In addition to the moral issue as to whether society has the right to take life, it also involves the question of whether it can act as a deterrent to offenders.

It is noteworthy that when the Article on the right to life was debated at the concluding session of the Constitutional Commission of Eritrea, the issue of capital punishment was raised, and a few members strongly expressed their opposition to it. The majority of the members of the Commission agreed with the provision of the draft constitution permitting the death penalty.

[Article 17(3), (4), (6)] (3) Doesn't lack of official languages make the requirement that every detainee shall be informed the grounds for his arrest or detention and his rights…in a language he understands difficult for the State?(4) If a person cannot be brought before a court of law within 48 hours of his arrest, this must be done as soon as possible thereafter. What does as soon as possible mean to the Commission? (6) People are entitled to a fair and public hearing. Making it public may be waived on the grounds of morals, public order and national security. Examples please?

17(3) The absence of official languages does not present any difficulties. The State is under an obligation to provide an interpreter to the accused.

17(4) As soon as possible means bringing the detainee within the shortest time possible, taking any available means of transporting the detainee to the place where the court is located—not a minute later. The usual reasons given for delay in our type of condition of underdeveloped infrastructure is lack of transport, and the extenuating circumstance such as flooding and impassable roads and bridges. The judge must take these reasons for delay into account.

17(6) The occasions when a court is asked to try a case in camera (as against in public view) are rare, accepted only when there are compelling reasons. To take the case of public security first, the prosecutor of a case involving evidence that may, if made public, adversely affect the security of the country, would be heard in camera. Similarly, in a case in which an open public trial may carry the risk of disorder by parties either in sympathy with, or opposed to, the accused, the court may decide to hold the trial out of public view. Finally, an example of a compelling reason related to morals in which the court may exclude the Press and the public. An example of exclusion of the Press and the public is where obscenity and child pornography is involved as well as situations where the court may wish to protect children from undue exposure and sustain mental or psychological harm.

[Article 18(1): "Every person shall have the right to privacy"] What does "right to privacy mean in the Eritrean context"?

Respect for a person's privacy is a universal human value. However, different cultures may reveal difference in emphasis regarding the enjoyment of the right to privacy. In the Eritrean, as in other African context, the emphasis on community interests has traditionally limited a strict application of the privacy principle. The community spirit historically defined by survival needs tends to dictate even the forms of social organization and the structure of the habitat. The form of their homesteads and other aspects of their infrastructure have tended to limit privacy with the submission of individuals and families to group intervention. Traditional values of mutual concern, of caring and sharing have tended to mediate between community interests and individual privacy. With the advent of "modernity," of individualism, the scale of values has begun to tip towards more privacy.

[Article 19(2), (3), (7)]19(2) What is "other media"? Does it include the Internet? 19(4) Do people have a right to practice "any" religion? 19(7) Why is the term "organizations" used and not "parties"? Are there limits on practicing "any profession," "any occupation or trade"?

19(2) Again, as with the case of Article 14(2) (discussed already), the resort to the exclusionary concept of "other media, other factors,…etc" is designed ensure that nothing else is excluded from coverage of the provision, in this instance freedom of expression. And yes, the Internet is definitely included.

19(4) Yes, people have the right to practice any religion. What is religion? This question may one day have to be defined either by the Legislature, or failing that, by the Supreme Court as the final arbiter of constitutional disputes.

19(7) "Organization" is a generic term that includes political parties as well as other political groups such as public forums that are formed as discussion facilitators without a political platform or ambition to election to public office. The controversy on this question is now mute since the decision by the current National Assembly to appoint a committee to draft a law on the formation and registration of political parties.

As for the question on limits to the practice of a profession, occupation or trade, this is answered by the insertion of the qualifying word "lawful." Any profession, occupation or trade that is not lawful, as defined by legislation, would be subject to legal sanctions.

[Article 20] Is the electoral law just drafted consistent with the constitution?

I will answer this in the next interview [Part IV] after I make a thorough a review of the draft law,

PART IV

I begin this portion of the interview, as I promised, by answering your question on whether the recently announced electoral law is consistent with the constitution. It is right, I think, that you should frame your question in terms of Article 20 of the constitution, which gives every Eritrean citizen the right to vote and to seek elective office. The constitution leaves to future legislation the details regarding the running for election and the rules and regulations incidental thereto. It lays down a condition that the exercise of the right to vote and to seek elective office is subject to the fulfillment of the requirements of the electoral law.

Is the draft law consistent with the constitution?

It depends on whether the law, in any way, limits or otherwise derogates from the right of a citizen seeking elective office, or the right of the voting citizen. Article 58 of the constitution provides for the establishment of an independent Electoral Commission with the responsibility (among other things) of ensuring that free and fair elections are held. The question whether the draft election law is consistent with the constitution will, therefore, turn principally on whether its provisions are such that fair and free elections can indeed be held. More specifically, the following questions need to be answered:

1. Will the Electoral Commission be independent: will it operate without the interference of the governing party, as the constitution requires?
2. Will there be a level playing field in which all the competing parties are treated equally, particularly in terms of financial resources?
3. Will the Media be accessible to all the candidates without favor?
4. Will they have sufficient time to organize their supporters and conduct their campaign, especially the new parties, if there are any?

I have reviewed the draft law on elections, together with the draft law on party formation. Does the draft election law pass the test in terms of the criteria listed above? Let us see:

First, on the independence of Electoral Commission, on the face of it, the draft law seems to follow the requirement of the constitution. Why do I inject a cautionary note by the qualifier "on the face of it"? Recall that we are talking about a highly competitive situation in which parties representing different interests and/or ideologies will compete for seats in the National assembly. Recall also that the said National Assembly elects the President of the country. According to the Constitution, the President appoints the Electoral Commission with the approval of the National Assembly. Now, in a post-constitutional implementation situation—in circumstances in which the National Assembly is composed of various political parties—the general practice is for the different parties to have their own nominees represented in the Electoral Commission. In the present instance, the National Assembly does not have such representation. The best that can be expected is for the nominating authority (the President) to have the good sense of including in the membership of the Electoral Commission respected people who are not members of PFDJ. The worst-case scenario is one in which the President appoints only members of PFDJ.

Let us assume that elections will be held, as announced, before the end of 2001 and there will be three major parties competing in the election. If PFDJ continues unreconstructed (and unrepentant) and one or more other parties compete for election to the National Assembly, the latter will be composed of PFDJ members with an overwhelming majority. Such a situation does not auger well for a democratic transition to constitutional government. There will be more loss of trust in government.

With respect to criteria numbers 2 and 3—equality of treatment in funding and access to the Media—the draft law follows standards set in most other countries. In our own case, however, the fact that the Media are owned by the government is a big minus because it can be susceptible to abuse in favor of a government candidate.

Criterion number 4 is crucial particularly to candidates of newly established parties. Government candidates would not only have the powerful backing of a well-heeled party and its enormous resources, they would most probably have better name recognition. The new candidates need much longer time, than the one contemplated in the draft law, to mount their campaigns, to get the message of their programs out and endeavor to persuade the public to elect them. They would need a minimum of three months.

In sum, there is much that is promising in the two draft laws, particularly the one on the formation of political parties. But, if the experience of the immediate past is any guide, I would not bet on a smooth ride to the democratic era that we have all been waiting for. There is, first of all, the matter of PFDJ' performance of the recent past which leaves much room to be desired. To be totally trusting of PFDJ's blandishments now, would be like the blind optimist undertaking a second marriage, reflecting the triumph of hope over experience, to borrow a phrase from Samuel Johnson.

Q. 18 [Article 22(2) and (3)] Do Sub-Articles 2 and 3 contradict each other?

I do not see any contradiction.

Q. 19 [Article 23] Does land belong to the State? To the Regions? To the people?

First, with respect to the ownership of land, Article 23(2) of the constitution provides that all land and all natural resources below and above the surface belong to the State. Second, the rights of citizens with regard to land have been determined by the Land Proclamation under which citizens have user (usufruct) rights both in urban and rural lands. According to the Proclamation, the traditional village communities have priority of rights over their agricultural land as well as land for building their houses. Third, the regions come into play as integral parts of the State in the administration, regulation and management of land issues.

Q. 20 [Article 25: Duties of Citizens]: If a citizen does not fulfill his/her duties under the constitution, is s/he not entitled to any rights? Some rights?

The relationship of constitutional rights and duties is not a zero sum game. To put it more prosaically, rights are rights, duties are duties. Rights are given to be protected and, when violated, the appropriate department of the State has a duty to redress any wrongs committed as a result of the violation of rights. And a breach of duty may carry some legal sanction, and any penalty attached to such breach must be administered in accordance with the law. In other words, a breach of duty does not lead to automatic suspension of rights without due process of law.

Although the three branches of government play their various roles in the protection of rights, it is the Judiciary that bears the major responsibility in redressing wrongs. It is worth underscoring the point that rights without duties would mean anarchy, just as duties without rights would amount to slavery. People tend to insist on their rights, and many do not always comply with their duties. The list of duties contained in Article 25 of the constitution are the most basic, considered so basic as to merit a place in the constitution. They are:

1. allegiance to the country,
2. defense of the country,

3. performing legally required national service,
4. advancing national unity,
5. respect and defense of the constitution
6. respecting the rights of others, and
7. complying with the requirements of the law.

A breach of any of these duties may lead to some sanctions, both legal and moral. The nature of the sanction will depend on the type of the duty and the circumstances under which the dereliction of duty occurred. It will also depend on the specificity with which the law respecting the particular duty has been defined.

And how does one enforce these duties? Can one contemplate the establishment of Inquisition type of institutions that would police the activities of citizens? Heaven Forbid! This would militate against citizens' fundamental rights. It is bad enough, as it is—what with self-appointed vigilantes rearing their ugly heads, sniffing for blood like attack dogs. We should rather simply expect that in a just and democratic society a culture of self-enforcing habits would develop to cultivate a proper sense of duty, which goes beyond the realm of law, even though there should be laws that provide for sanctions against breach of duties. But, as already noted, breach of duties should never automatically lead to suspension of rights. Even a deserter from the war front, as bad as his action may be, must have his day in court with due process of law applied scrupulously and with his innocence presumed until the contrary is proven.

Q. 21 [Article 26]: The loopholes allowing the State to limit fundamental rights and freedoms are only those consistent with a "just and democratic society." But isn't that phrase controversial and open to interpretation?

The limitation on the fundamental rights and freedoms of citizens rests on the philosophical assumption that there is no absolute right that cannot be limited under any circumstances. This assumption is shared by all constitutional systems. What Article 26 does, then, is to lay down criteria for courts to apply when called upon to decide under what conditions a limitation on a fundamental right will be valid and acceptable. The courts must be satisfied that the measures taken are necessary in a just and democratic society. Both "just" and "democratic" are to be determined by discerning judges.

A comparative perspective may be helpful. For instance, the US constitution does not have an equivalent Article, but US courts have developed guiding principles similar to the ones listed under Article 26 of the Eritrean constitution. The Canadian constitution places fundamental human rights subject to "such reasonable limits prescribed by law as can be demonstrably justified in a free and democratic society." The South African constitutional's formula is that the limitation must be "reasonable" and "justifiable in an open and democratic society based on freedom and equality."

Q. 22 [Article 27]: Should we have declared a state of emergency in the war with Ethiopia?

Article 27(1) of the constitution gives the President the power to declare a state of emergency. It is one of the exclusive powers of the President, with the proviso that the declaration will not be effective unless approved by a resolution passed by a two-thirds majority of the National Assembly. Whether the President should have declared a state of emergency in the war with Ethiopia, I cannot say. I do not think it is fair to second-guess the President's decision in this particular instance. A declaration of a state of emergency has political as well as legal implications in terms of limiting citizens' rights. But I do think that there should have been full disclosure of the creeping crisis between the two countries that ended up in the outbreak of a full-scale war in May 1998. The president should have held consultations with the National Assembly and members of his cabinet on the evolving problem, long before the situation exploded into war. Citizens have a right to be informed of such critical events and developments so that all avenues of peaceful settlement of the disputes could be explored and openly debated. Full disclosure, open public debate, and exposure of the suffering of Eritrean victims of the creeping crisis on all fronts might have induced caution on the part of the aggressor party and led to a negotiated settlement of the crisis.

Q. 23 [28]: There are people in jail, right now, who haven't had the benefit of a constitutional due process. The only remedy for them is the court. But can we expect judges, all of whom are PFDJ members, to be so impartial to rule against the government?

Your question is posed in relation to Article 28 of the constitution, which deals with the enforcement of fundamental rights and freedoms. The answer to the questions as to who enforces these rights and freedoms, and who defends them or ensures that their violation is sanctioned is given by the constitution itself. First, and foremost, the citizens have the duty to observe them and to act as watchdog for their observance. The Article on the duties of citizens, as we have seen, includes the duty to respect and defend the constitution as well as to respect the rights of others. The second line of defense and, institutionally speaking, the most effective, is the judiciary. The courts must follow the provisions of the constitution as the source of government legitimacy and the basis of the protection of the rights, freedoms and dignity of citizens and of just administration. The courts are not only entitled but by duty bound to rectify wrongs and to order at their discretion and award of monetary compensation in favor of a complainant, where it is found that an award is justifiable.

Does the fact that the majority (not all) of the judges are PFDJ members affect their impartiality? It may, it may not, depending on the individual judge. There may be some diehard members of the PFDJ who may not act independently without fear or favor, as they are required to do under their oath of judicial service. I would be surprised, however, if that represents the majority of the judges. My sense is that even the card-carrying members of PFDJ regard their judicial duties as separate from their duties as party members. In fact, this is one of the challenges facing law teachers and students to monitor and on which to do some serious research. Legal education and research is critical in our situation not only in terms of imparting knowledge but also in raising the level of consciousness of those engaged in the judicial service.

Part V

[Article 31] Does the constitution envision full-time legislators? How many months of the year will the Assembly be in session? How many are the members of the Assembly?

Legislators are expected to work on a full-time basis, with ample time for them to spend among their constituents. The constitution leaves to future legislation to determine the length of the sessions as well as other details on the organization of the work of the Assembly. The number of the members of the National Assembly will be determined on the basis of a census, but if I were to give a rough estimate, it would probably be somewhere between 150 and 160. In 1997, before the ratification of the constitution, the Transitional National Assembly had 150 members, consisting of 75 PFDJ members of the Central Council, and 75 members of the Regional Assemblies.

[Article 32(8) (10)] (8) Why is there a requirement for "absolute majority of all its members" in electing a President whereas a 2/3 vote is required to impeach and remove? (10) The National assembly "may approve" or "must approve" the appointment of any person?

Originally, a two-thirds majority was considered by the Commission, following the antecedent of the UN-imposed, 1952 constitution. The issue of the vote required to elect a President was debated in the larger context of the choice of the mixed system that the Commission adopted. If you look at the US system of executive presidency, the President is elected by the citizens, albeit through the archaic mechanism of the Electoral College. By contrast, the parliamentary model—what we can call the Westminster model—the Prime Minister is the leader of the party that obtains majority seats in the Parliament. Eritrea adopted a mixed system that combines parts of the two systems. The inspirational source was Eritrea's experience both under the 1952 constitution and the "government" during the latter part of the liberation struggle. In terms of the new democratic constitutional system, the Commission anticipated the emergence of multi-parties and democratic politics that will inevitably be "messy," if more interesting and necessary. In such eventuality, obtaining a two-thirds majority may be hard—even conceivably impossible—to obtain. This would lead to constitutional crisis. No nation, least of all, a developing nation like Eritrea, should be subjected to such crisis. Hence, the decision to avoid a two-thirds majority.

On the other hand, the removal and impeachment of a President being a very serious matter needs a two-thirds majority. To require a less stringent standard would lay the country to the risk of politically motivated resort to demands for impeachment and thus to institutional instability.

(10) The wording of this Sub-Article is clear. It says the National Assembly "shall have the power to approve an appointment pursuant to this constitution." SHALL," not "may"

[Article 33] What happens if the President does not sign a "draft law within 30 days"

If he does not sign within 30 days, the National Assembly would request him to fulfill his constitutional obligation and sign the Bill into law. The Assembly would do this through the office of its Chairman. If the President has good reasons for not signing the Bill into law, he must explain within a reasonably short time. If those reasons are not accepted by the Assembly, the latter would insist on the Bill being signed into law. If the President refuses or delays the signing of the Bill, the National Assembly would issue a formal resolution condemning such refusal and indicating that if its request is not accepted within a given time limit, it may start impeachment proceedings against the President pursuant to Articles 32(9) and 41(6) of the constitution. Article 32(9) gives the National Assembly the power to impeach the President, and Article 41(6) lays down the grounds on which it may impeach him/her. One of the reasons for which the President may be impeached, or impeached and charged, is for violation of the constitution. Refusal to sign a draft law is a violation of Article 33 of the constitution, which imposes a mandatory duty on the President to sign a draft law sent to him by the National assembly. It would be a foolish President indeed that would persist in such obdurate behavior.

[Article 34] Is the Chairman of the National Assembly the equivalent of the US Speaker of the House? If he, too, is voted in by an absolute majority of all its members, does the constitution envision creating two strong co-leaders of the State? But he cannot vote except in cases of a tie?

Yes, the Chairman is equivalent to the US Speaker of the House. The Chairman of the National Assembly succeeds the President in the event of a vacancy in the office of the President. [See Article 41(4)] He is, thus, next to the President, the most important State official. Be that as it may, it does not mean that there are two "strong co-leaders" of the State. It means that the leader of the National Assembly enjoys the high honor and prestige commensurate with the oversight powers of the National Assembly that he heads.

[Article 39] Why is the President the Head of State, Head of Government and Commander-in-Chief? Why is the President not elected directly by the people?

The executive of a State has dual functions, the one representing the nation as a whole, the other heading the government of the day. In principle, the role of the Head of State is to be above the fray of politics, but to live with the outcome of the political process and mediate in situations of conflict that may have far-reaching implications to the integrity of the State. In the constitutions of some countries exemplified by the US constitutions the President is both Head of State and Head of the government, and Commander-in-Chief.

In the constitutions of other countries, the two functions are performed by two different people. In such a case the Head of State—be he/she king/queen, or president—performs ceremonial, and mediation and custodial functions. For example, in the constitution of Ireland, the President is the custodian of the constitution and, as such, has the right to check legislation to see if it conforms to the constitution. In this kind of divided executive system, executive power (real power) is vested in the Prime Minister who is head of government by virtue of the majority his party enjoys in the Parliament.

The President of Eritrea is like the US President in that he combines the two functions of Head of State and Head of government. He is also like the Prime Minister in a divided executive system in that he derives his power from his election by the National Assembly. And because he combines the power of both offices, he naturally becomes Commander-in-Chief.

As to the question why he is not elected by the people, it is interesting to report that, during the public debate phase of the constitution making process, Eritreans living in the United States, for the most part, preferred the US type of election. By contrast, Eritreans living in Europe, which have the parliamentary system, preferred the system adopted by the Commission in which the President is elected by the Legislature.

[Article 41(1) (3) (5)] (1) How did you arrive at the 20% minimum threshold to nominate a member to the presidency? (3) Why did you decide on term limits? Doesn't this infringe on people's right to choose whom they want? (5) Let's say a member is elected to the presidency. Within one month, he resigns or dies in office. The Chairman of the National assembly becomes president. Let's say he is elected to the presidency. This person can serve as president for 15 years short one month. Doesn't the create opportunity for mischief? Once a legislator is elected to be president, is his seat filled by an appointment, special election or does it remain vacant?

(Sub. 1) The Commission thought it wise to have reasonable threshold for nomination of the President in order to avoid or minimize fractious politicking including frivolous attempts at the Presidency. To those ends, it arrived at the 20 % as being a reasonable minimum. The arithmetic of election politics is always subject to controversy. What is at issue here?

Assume that the members of the National Assembly are 165. 20 percent of 165 is 33. This means that a maximum of five candidates can divide up between them in numbers satisfying the minimum threshold. Let us say there are five candidates, each with no less than 33 people nominating them, the voting will have to be repeated until one of them obtains a $2/3^{rd}$ majority of the 165 members, i.e., 110 votes. The idea behind this political arithmetic is to end the politics of domination and exclusion and, instead, to encourage a healthy politics of give and take in which the majority party will be forced to accommodate the views and interests of minority parties. The politics of consensus will develop out of such situation. Democracy is "messy", but as it has been aptly said, all the others have been tried and found to be wanting.

(Sub. 3) Two concerns are juxtaposed in this question: the value of term limits on the one hand and the right of the voters to choose whom they want. In the opinion of the Commission, the former far outweighs the latter. The Commission's decision to have term limits is based on the conviction, based on experience and a reading of history, that staying too long in power tends to result in the corruption of leaders with all the attendant problems. There are two kinds of corruption. One is financial corruption; the other is political corruption involving the abuse or misuse of power. The two are linked in that the latter leads to the former. Presidency without term limit creates the illusion of invincibility and results in arrogance, and abuse follows such illusion even as the day follows the night. We cannot repeat too often British historian Lord Acton's dictum that power tends to corrupt and absolute power corrupts absolutely. Additionally, term limits impose an obligation on political leaders the duty to groom successors, which in turn encourages peaceful succession. And peaceful succession is crucial to the healthy development of a nation.

I would like to inject here a personal note. Quite frankly, I did not expect the PFDJ leadership to accept the idea of term limits; and I was gearing up to do battle when I and two of my colleagues of the Executive Committee of the Commission were summoned to the meeting of the National Assembly at the time it was debating the final draft of the constitution. Someone in the Assembly raised the question why we should have term limits. As I recall, it was one of the members of the inner circle of PFDJ. And to my utter surprise, the President who was chairing the meeting admonished him and gave a cogent reason why there should be term limits. From that point onwards, I relaxed and began to enjoy the rest of the meeting and left with understandable satisfaction. I was so impressed and gratified that, immediately after the event, I went home and wrote a poem of praise (Qine Mewedis) in our classical language—romantic creature that I am!

This raises the question whether the President believed in what he was saying? I thought so at the time and only began to entertain some doubts with the postponement of the implementation of the constitution. We must now leave this and other related questions to the judgment of history.

(Sub. 5) In the extremely unlikely event that a president resigns or dies in office one month after his election and the Chairman of the National Assembly succeeds him, two things must be done. First, the National Assembly Chairman automatically fills the vacancy, on an interim basis, for one month. Then the Assembly must elect a new President, which can be the Assembly Chairman or someone else, depending on how the Assembly evaluates the Chairman. If the Chairman is elected and runs for election successfully in the next two terms, it means your hypothetical fear is realized—one person will have been President for ten years and eleven months, eleven months more than the allotted term limit.

Well, if that should happen, it would be seen as an exception that proves the rule. You wonder if that might create opportunity for mischief. What kind of mischief? The kind in which Caesar's friends—Brutus, Cassius and the others—conspired to assassinate Caesar? My answer is that for every Brutus and Cassius, there is a Mark Anthony to avenge Caesar and after avenging him cry: "Mischief thou art afoot. Take thou what course thou wilt."

It is not possible to provide for every conceivable eventuality, in constitutional engineering, as in much else in life. There are many things that must be left to the working of the political process, and this is one of them. If mischief is attempted one would hope that the good sense of the citizens and members of the National Assembly would let them do the right thing in response.

The answer to the question what happens to the seat left vacant by the election of one of the Assembly's member to the Presidency is simply that it remains vacant, as does the seat of the Prime Minister in a parliamentary government. Theoretically, the President, as an elected member of the National Assembly, can sit in Parliament. But because it is a hybrid system, as I said earlier, the President, as an Executive Chief and Head of State must remain aloof and above the parliamentary process. This is a unique system and needs to be considered as such.

[Article 46(2)] If the President picks his entire cabinet from the Assembly, are replacements appointed, elected or do they, too, remain vacant?

The reason why Article 46 gives the President power to appoint ministers either from among the members of the National Assembly or from outside of the Assembly was to enable him/her to tap on as many sources as possible. The pool of talent, experience and expertise required for ministerial appointment may not be available among the members of the assembly. Now, if the President be so foolish as to pick all his ministers from the Assembly, irrespective of the requisite qualifications, the Ministers' seats would not be filled by election or appointment; the Ministers will remain members and attend its meetings when required to do so pursuant to the rules and regulations (to be) issued by the Assembly. In their case, classical parliamentary rule should apply.

[Article 49(4)]: Why did the CCE (the Commission) leave designating the tenure of the justices of the Supreme Court to the Legislators?

Concerning the judiciary, the most important principle is its independence from the direction and control of any person or authority, as ordained by Article 48(2) and (3). Judges shall be subject only to the law, to a judicial code of conduct determined by law and their conscience. The security of their tenure is a critical factor in ensuring such independence. Therefore, the legislators, in deliberating the law concerning the tenure of judges and other conditions of their service, must keep this constitutional principle in mind. If they don't, the interpretive power of the Supreme Court should apply in striking down a law that falls short of the constitution's requirement. This is also an area in which the citizens' role as the first line of defense in the enforcement of constitutional rights should be brought to bear; citizens can pressure their members of Parliament to pass a law that ensures judicial independence.

PART VI

Response to Awate Readers' Questions: Dear Readers: This is the final part of our interview with Dr. Bereket. It deal with final questions; some follow-up questions to previous answers as well as questions forwarded by readers.

Accronyms:

CCE: Constitutional Commission of Eritrea
EPLF: Eritrean People's Liberation Front
PFDJ: People's Front for Democracy and Justice
PIA: President Isias Afwerki
ELF: Eritrean Liberation Front

Jamal Almualem's question concerns the autonomy of the Constitutional Commission of Eritrea (CCE). He asks if the claim of CCE's autonomy is valid, then why is it that what "PIA had said before drafting the constitution found their way to the constitution?" Jamal cites, as examples, Eritrean official languages, and the formation of political parties "to the exact specification of EPLF."

I repeat that the constitution was not written to the specification of the EPLF, although the EPLF, or the PFDJ since February 1994, was duly consulted on a number of issues, as a governing party. As I said repeatedly during the constitution making process, a governing party has every right to be consulted, but that is different from such a party or its government dictating to the constitution making entity. If the ELF had been the government, instead of the EPLF, it too would have been duly consulted. The autonomy of CCE was never compromised at any time during the three-year period of constitutional consultation. There were perhaps two or three occasions when PIA raised questions on the manner and direction of the Commission's conduct of its business, let alone dictate to it. For he knew that if he tried, I would hand in my resignation.

The essence of the new politics of constitution making—the Constitutional Commission method—is that the Commission, once appointed, must be autonomous. The fact that the views of the Commission coincided with that of the government in no way impugns the autonomy of the Commission or the integrity of the process. If Jamal or others do not agree with this, so be it; they are entitled to their views.

With respect to the question of official languages, as I explained previously, the recommendation of the Commission coincided with the preferred option of EPLF/PFDJ, that option being simply declaring the equality of all Eritrean languages and continuing with Arabic and Tigrigna as working languages, but not as official languages. Declaring any language(s) as official derogates from the principle of equality of languages, which is a cardinal principle. This is a continuation of the EPLF's long-held policy originating from the years of the armed struggle and, as members of that armed struggle, the majority of the Commission were evidently influenced by that policy. I do not pretend to know what the policy of the ELF was on the question of language, but I do recall that during the debate on this issue, several former ELF members who participated in the debates strongly urged that Arabic and Tigrigna be declared as official languages. I notice in the recent debate on the issue of languages some prominent Eritrean intellectuals argue in favor of such a policy. Now, if the majority of the people of Eritrea were to seek a revision of the constitution demanding that Arabic and Tigrigna be made official languages, reverting to the UN-imposed constitutional provision, then that would have to be tabled as a question for constitutional amendment in accordance with Article 59 of the constitution.

In the meantime, I would argue that the present policy of declaring the equality of languages is a wise and reasonable one. I will not repeat here what I have already covered, in defense of that policy, but I take this opportunity to answer a question that I had overlooked in response to Saleh A.A. Younis's earlier question as to the difference between official and working languages. The answer to that question is that, in terms of practical application, there is no difference, but that the official status of a language carries with it legal implications. Such implications include the requirement that all government business must be conducted in the official language(s), that all official acts and laws must be published in the official language(s), and that speakers of the language and other interested parties can demand, as a matter of legal right, that all this be done.

Jamal also claims that the Commission's position on the formation of political parties reflects PIA's position. I have answered this question in a different context in previous answers to questions posed by the interviewer, Saleh Younis. The constitution provides that citizens have a right to form political organizations; a term that includes political parties, contrary to the denial of this by some commentators. That this term includes political parties has been confirmed by events since October 2000. The Transitional National Assembly of Eritrea passed a Resolution on October 2, 2000 correctly interpreting the constitution's provision on this subject, and establishing a committee to draft a law on the formation of political parties. As everyone now knows, PIA dismissed the chairman of the said committee because the latter began to do what the National Assembly mandated it to do, namely organize public consultations before submitting the draft law to the National Assembly.

It is quite obvious that PIA feared the Committee would act autonomously (as the Constitutional Commission did) in conducting a public consultation process. Some of the prominent members of the Committee had already made it clear that there needs to be alternative parties and the committee chairman's actions in defiance of PIA's strictures indicated that the committee had indeed decided to challenge PIA's dominance of Eritrean political life by insisting on open public debate that would facilitate the emergence of other parties. What will come out of this politics of dominance versus reform is not known. If the past is any guide, PIA and his PFDJ stalwarts will try to whip up support among the captive masses for their version and conduct an election to their liking. Whether PIA allows other parties to challenge PFDJ and, if he does, what impact such party will have on Eritrea's future politics remains to be seen. But since the challenge posed by the "reformist group" comprising the most prominent and popular leaders of the EPLF, Eritrean politics as we have known it has changed. I sincerely hope that PIA has the good sense to change his obdurate ways and listen to his former comrades-in-arms, for the sake of the nation.

A reader who did not reveal his name asked me the following four questions: (a) Do I believe that the "EPDJ" (sic) started the war?(b) Do I believe that an ordinary Eritrean should hold me accountable "for not defining the date for the implementation of the constitution…" that I chaired? (c) -Is this interview censored? If not, is there any chance of broadcasting the interview in internet audio (realplay format)? (d) -What would my stance be in regard to Eritrea if the Haile Selassie regime were still in power?

I will answer the question whether I believe that the PFDJ started the war, later [in the next and final part of this interview, Part VI, B] together with the other personal questions.

The answer to the second question is definitely yes; I have said so in a previous posting (in Asmarino.com) on the subject of the implementation of the Eritrean constitution. I cannot do better than to repeat what I wrote in that posting. I said:

"…But promises have been made and easily broken in the past, including the undertaking to put the constitution into effect soon after its ratification. The Constitutional Commission of Eritrea opted not to include an article in that constitution mentioning a date for its coming into effect on the strength of such implicit understanding. In retrospect, it was a mistake for which the Commission, and I personally as its chairman, must take responsibility. It was a mistake based on trust. There is a commercial ad of an insurance company showing the picture of a little child touching the base of the horn of a rhinoceros. The caption reads: 'Trust is not being afraid even if you're vulnerable.' The Commission chose not to be afraid, even though it was vulnerable to betrayal. It made a decision based on trust, and has been living the consequences."

I will let the Awate team answer the details of the third question. As to whether this interview was censored, I certainly did not do any censoring, and I did not experience any censoring on the part of interviewer.

The fourth question is a strange one. What would my stance be in regard to Eritrea if the Haile Selassie regime were still in power today?! I refer the person who asked these questions to the first interview of these series. The assumption of his question, I take it, is that I might conceivably entertain a different attitude towards Haile Selassie's government today. Think of it—I resigned from that government in 1964, ten years before the regime tottered and fell. Why would I entertain any different attitude towards a regime from which I resigned in protest, long before Eritrea gained its independence, an independence that I cherish, and devoted a major part of my adult life to help achieve?

Daniel asks two questions: (a) What steps are being taken to strengthen the legal system at present, in particular the commercial law? (b) -Are there provisions in the constitution such rights as the right to take the government to court?

First, the legal system. You may know, Daniel, that Eritrea's modern legal system is derived from its colonizers. The Italians superimposed their commercial and public law (Administrative, Constitutional and Commercial laws) on their colony's various traditional laws. The last colonizer, Ethiopia, imposed on Eritrea its laws, which were derived from foreign sources. These are: the Civil Code, drafted by a French professor, the Criminal Code drafted by a Swiss professor, etc.

Upon Eritrea's liberation, the Provisional Government of Eritrea made certain amendments to these laws but kept the bulk of them as received. But over the past few years, the Ministry of justice has been engaged in developing new codes of law: a criminal code, a criminal procedure code and a commercial code. The first two are ready for consideration by the legislature, but whether the government will submit them to the transitional National Assembly or wait until a new Parliament is elected on the basis of the constitution is an open question. Nobody knows. The public is kept in the dark, as usual.

The latest word on the commercial code is that a first draft was presented to the ministry, but there have been some criticisms on it and it has been temporarily shelved, or is being reconsidered with the addition of new drafters.

The revision (or development) of the civil code will take much longer time. The civil code is much more complex, embracing many different topics touching on practically all aspects of the lives of the citizens.

Finally, two points need to be made, one on the constitution, and another on the legal personnel of Eritrea. On the first point, it cannot be overstressed that the implementation of the constitution is a prerequisite for the development of the legal system. The constitution is the ultimate point of reference of all legal issues and the final arbiter of all disputes. On the question of the legal personnel, we all know that Eritrea does not have nearly enough legally trained people. The few that are legally trained and experienced are horrifically overburdened, inadequately equipped and poorly paid. The opening of the Law School at Asmara University has started to ease the burden somewhat with the first batch of graduates of the LL.B degree starting to work. We have a long way to go before we reach a critical mass of legal personnel to staff the courts and other legal offices.

The second question can be answered by simple yes. Please read the Bill of Rights of the constitution. (Chapter 3.) If the government or any member of the government violates any of the rights listed in chapter three, a citizen can sue in a court of law, which raises the question of the independence of the judiciary. "In the exercise of judicial power, the courts shall be free from the direction and control of any person or authority. Judges shall be subject only to the law, to a judicial code of conduct determined by law and to their conscience." (Article 48(2). The constitution also enjoins all organs of the Sate to accord the courts "such assistance as they may require to protect their independence and dignity so that they may exercise their judicial power appropriately and effectively pursuant to the provisions of the constitution."

B.A. asks a question based on my article, "The Disappearance of the Eritrean Constitution" (posted in Asmarino.com). In that article I had stated that the Commission's Executive Committee had discussed, in one of its last meetings, the so-called corruption laws which were in violation of some provisions of the constitution. The laws provide for special courts with exclusive jurisdiction over crimes of corruption. One of the clauses of these laws denies the accused the right of appeal, which violates Article 17(8) of the constitution and is contrary to traditional norms of justice. B.A. asks me: (a) What was my personal reaction then and now? (b) Is it possible to make changes in this unfair law that was made by the GOE? and (c) Am I willing to challenge this unreasonable anti-corruption law?

The answer to (a) is that I was against the law then, and I am now. The dilemma I and my colleagues at the Constitutional Commission faced was a fait accompli of a law, which came as a surprise even to some of government insiders. The law was there; all we could do was express our disagreement with it and strongly urge the government to change it and to speed up the docket of cases pending in the special courts established under this law. As I already said, the Commission withheld the option of fixing an effective date for the coming into force of the constitution in order to give the government time to clear the deck, so to speak. It was a mistake made on the basis of trust. And this is a great lesson to all would-be constitution makers.

The answer to (b) is: Not only is it possible to change the law, the government is under an obligation to live by the constitution and must thus change the law. I have speculated in the cited article that it is the government' reluctance to change the law that caused it to postpone the implementation of the constitution. And why does it refuse to change the law? Presumably because it has not been able to dispose of the pending cases of corruption, and because the government believes the law is a deterrent against corruption! Deterrent, or no deterrent, the constitution comes first, and the government has no choice now but the abolition of this law.

The answer to © is that I have already challenged the law as being in violation of the constitution. I would like to know what else needs to be done in that regard. Everyone I have talked to, beginning from the Chief Justice and lawyers in the Ministry of Justice, and all observers, foreign and domestic, are opposed to this monstrosity of a law. The detention, without trial, of so many Eritreans, including heroic freedom fighters, does not stand to reason or logic.

Two explanations have been advanced to try to make sense of this law. One is that PIA believes that the law has stemmed the tide of corruption and that he is willing to accept the charge of acting contrary to the constitution in his the fight against corruption. I am sure that this is what he believes. If so, he has to make up his mind: either he lives by the word of the constitution, or he does not. If he does not, he stands the risk of being impeached one day pursuant to Articles 32(9), and 41(6). The other explanation is that PIA is a "control freak" and is using the law as weapon of control over government and party cadres. The truth may lie somewhere in between these two explanations, but whatever the real reason, PIA has created a monster that he needs to dispose of—and soon.

Temesghen Tsegay asks several questions: The first is divided into two: (a) "when you introduced the constitution how much did our people participate in percentage? and (b) did the government of the EPLF pressure the committee (he means the Commission)? If yes, for what reason?

The answer to (a) is twofold. First, during the first phase of the constitution making process (1994-1995) over half a million Eritreans participated in civic education seminars and debates. Of these some 40 per cent were women. This number includes Eritreans in the Diaspora who played a major role in this as they did during the armed struggle. The seminars and related debates during this phase were based on the Proposals that the Commission had prepared having consulted with the public and with experts.

Second, during the third phase (1996-1997), the seminars and public debates were based on the draft constitution prepared by the Commission. During this phase over 127,000 Eritreans participated in the debate on the constitutional draft. Again, Eritreans in the Diaspora participated in this phase.

The answer to (b) is that the government did not apply any direct pressure on the Commission. Attempts were made to influence the members of the Commission to accept the idea of "guided democracy" with the implied suggestion of accepting a one party state. This was not acceptable to the Commission. As a lawyer/social scientist, I was fascinated by such subtle attempts which reflect the continuation of the practice of "democratic centralism" of the earlier days which had it its uses during the armed struggle, but which was a discredited mode of political practice. The dialectic at work, between the remnants of democratic centralism on the one hand, and liberal democratic theory and praxis on the other, was of immense interest to me, not only as practitioner, heading the drafting of the constitution, but as an interested academic. We started with a "bill of goods," as it were, clearly and boldly advocating democracy, the rule of law and human rights. We translated several international legal instruments, including the Universal Declaration of Human Rights of

1948, and the 1966 UN Covenants on political social economic and cultural rights into Eritrean vernaculars and broadcast them over the radio and distributed them before the start of the public seminars. These "bill of goods" were the ramparts which no "democratic centralist" could penetrate. The rest was a matter of management of the conduct of the process, which went very well, by all independent accounts. [It may be of interest to Temesgen and others that we prepared and published a 50+ page handbook in Tigrigna and Arabic (Meba'ta Qiwam=Introduction to the Constitution).] It became an indispensable tool for members of the Commission and for the 400 people we trained to help conduct public seminars.]

Temesgen's second question is about the aims of the G 13. The aim of the G 13 is set forth clearly and concisely in the Berlin letter, which is now available in both Arabic and Tigrigna. I am answering this question here, as being relevant under A, because one of the requests of the G 13 was for the immediate implementation of the constitution.

Temesgen's third question refers to the recently drafted laws on political parties and election. He asks my opinion on the two laws. I have answered this question in one of the interviews with Saleh Younis. In my view, the draft law on political parties is a good one although it may need some refinement. The electoral law leaves much room to be desired. I refer Temesgen to the answers I gave to the interview. It is possible that he sent the questions before that particular interview.

His fourth question asks me if I will participate in the next election, and if I win, what do I do in my four year terms. Although this is a personal question and belongs in B, the next section, I will answer it because the answer is a simple one. I am not interested in any political office, elective or otherwise. After half a life-time of active public service, I can now serve better as a free citizen, offering critical support.

The Fifth question says: "What do we respect (expect?) from the next election? How do you compare the Eritrean people?" He adds a sixth question: "As you are an educated man what do you advise us?"

The next election, even if PIA sees fit to allow other parties to compete will probably be won by him and his party. The cards are stacked against opposition parties. PFDJ is a powerful, well-funded party and its leaders have name recognition and control the instrument of state power, particularly the Media. But if other parties are allowed to compete, however weak they are, their advent will be like the acorn that can grow into an oak tree one day. The question is will PIA and company allow this.

The Eritrean people are a wonderful people—heroic, loyal, hard working and patient. They have sacrificed much to attain our independence, and lately, to maintain it. In response to the question what advise I can give, I would say, above all, we owe it to these wonderful people, to the martyrs and their orphans and widows, and to those who have been handicapped by the war, to maintain our unity as a people. We must do this, even as we debate and argue about different issues and criticize our government. We also need to keep the light of liberty and democracy burning and make those who govern us accountable for their actions and omissions. We need to practice tolerance as the first requirement of the democratic imperative. To those who are critical of the way the constitution was made, I say, give it a chance and if it is found wanting in practice, organize to introduce amendments to accommodate your ideas or desires.

At this critical juncture of our history, our domestic politics is witnessing two forces that are facing each other—the forces of reform and those with vested interests in maintaining the status quo. Every Eritrean needs to ask himself/herself which side he/she supports and why. Above all, each one must do everything to see to it that the face-off is resolved democratically: that it does not degenerate into violence, as seems to be happening in Ethiopia.

These are the words not so much of "an educated man", to use Temesgen's phrase, as those of an elder who has seen much—both good and bad—and wishes his country and people nothing but the best.

And I wish to take this opportunity to wish all Eritreans:

HAPPY TENTH INDEPENDENCE ANNIVERSARY!!!!!!!!

End of interview.

AWATE.COM, *BEREKET H SELASSE*, *CONSTITUTION*, *ERITREA*, *INTERVIEW*
SHARE

PART III
THE RULE OF LAW AND ITS PLACE IN ERITREA'S AGENDA OF DEMOCRACY BUILDING AND THE ROLE OF PARLIAMENT UNDER THE ERITREAN CONSTITUTION

The Rule of Law and the Administration of Justice

A Paper Presented at the Conference on
Building Democracy in Eritrea
London, April 24-25, 2019

By
Bereket Habte Selassie

I. Introduction: The Rule of Law and its Misadventure in Eritrea

In the annals of the history of fighting for establishing the principle of the rule of law, in Eritrea, what is known as the "Berlin letter" must take a special place. This is so because the letter highlighted the Rule of Law—or rather its suppression—as a primary issue of concern. The letter made a strong plea to President Isaias asking him to implement the constitution and apply the rule of law. The authors of the letter wrote, among other things, that they were "dismayed to witness the operation of institutions that are clearly and flagrantly in violation of the spirit and letter of the (1997) constitution." The letter continues:

> "We are astounded to hear of practices that are contrary to the provisions of the constitution continue today. We, therefore, solemnly request you to take the necessary steps to ensure the full and immediate implementation of our constitution. As a sign of good will and seriousness of intent, again, we would like you to abolish the 'special court' which is undermining the rule of law and creating disaffection among a segment of our population."

> *[See Appendix I of Wounded Nation: How a Once Promising ERITREA was Betrayed and its Future Compromised, Bereket Habte Selassie, Red Sea Press (2011)].*

The authors of the Berlin letter (reproduced in the aforementioned Appendix I of Wounded Nation...) urged the President to release, or bring before a court of law, people who have been detained for many years, without trial. They end the letter by pledging to engage in efforts "to promote a culture of openness, tolerance, accountability and the rule of law." To those ends, they expressed their intention to broaden their base by convening a larger meeting which would consider the President's response to their letter. The idea was to begin and institutionalize "a government/civil society dialogue on a continuing basis as a critical part of a healthy development of our future."

Little did they suspect that Isaias had decided to dispense with the idea altogether. In all innocence they assumed he was on the same ideological wavelength as theirs—one that embraced the Rule of Law and democracy—when he wrote the group a letter expressing his desire to meet with them any time, anywhere. They decided to go to Asmara, rather than insist on meeting him abroad, out of deference to him and respect for the office of President. As is now well known, the President's response during his meeting with the group in Asmara was not encouraging, to put it mildly. Nor has there been any movement on the part of his government to abolish the "special court" or to bring the detainees to court. Clearly, the man had abandoned all pretense of establishing a constitutional system of government, contrary to his promise and in violation of the solemn resolution of two congresses of the EPLF, the party that he led.

In a previous essay that I wrote (*on line in an Eritrean website*), under the title of "*The disappearance of the Eritrean constitution*" I had expressed surprise to learn that some members of the leadership of PFDJ (the successor of EPLF) had a cavalier attitude towards the rule of law. And I had objected to the existence of the "special court" after the ratification of the constitution, as well as the continued detention of people without being given the right to appear before an ordinary court of law. I was shocked to learn that the President chose not to respond to the pleas of the authors of the Berlin letter and other similar voices. I said that this did not augur well for the rule of law. I reminded all concerned of the oath of office of the President as well as other provisions of the constitution that enjoin him to "uphold and defend the constitution," and that he is the preeminent guardian of the constitution and should therefore ensure that the rule of law—the soul of a constitutional system—be applied.

All this was long before we lost our innocence as a nation and that worse things were to happen very soon. Not long after that, when asked why he did not implement the constitution, Isaias answered shamelessly and with sarcasm that the constitution was "just a piece of paper." And finally, he proclaimed to the astonishment of the Eritrean nation and the world that the constitution is dead. By that time, it had become clear to all of us that **"our president" saw himself as a king, and that as such he was above the law.** The freedom fighter that had led a heroic group of fellow freedom fighters, and who had promised to help ensure the introduction of a democratic form of government and to abide by the constitution and the rule of law, had betrayed his trust and decided to rule Eritrea like a king, unaccountable to anybody.

Fast forward to the Summer of 2018.

Isaias Afwerki's behavior following the political change in Ethiopia in the Summer of 2018, marks a complete break with the past during which he had pretended to follow the resolution of the EPLF, the Front that he led. The new behavior represents clear manifestation of his abandonment of all pretense of following any democratic process, a process in which crucial decisions affecting a nation ought to be made by some mechanism involving the people or their representatives. The fact that Isaias did not even consult his own hand-picked cabinet Ministers in all this extraordinary adventure of one-man dealings with the Ethiopian Prime Minster, signing serious agreements involving the Fate and fortune of a nation, is nothing short of catastrophic. How Isaias has been able to do this and get away with it should be a matter for serious analysis by all concerned. It demands that we Eritreans as a people need to look deeply into ourselves and wonder how we have allowed one man to get away with so much so easily, violating a constitutional obligation and a solemn resolution of the EPLF at two Congresses.

[Historical analysis is not adequate in such review; More importantly, it should include a professional psychiatrist to explain Isaias Afwerki's behavior].

Incidentally, Eritrea is not unique in such historical phenomenon in which one man of dubious character is allowed to get away "with murder" so to speak. In the United States of America, the ease with which a racist, misogynist, serial liar and con man has been able to impress a sufficient number of electors to vote for him in the 2016 presidential election is a cautionary tale in democratic politics in our time. Indeed, Trump's advent and his two-year record of chaos and confusion in American politics must be a source of gratification for all autocrats and impostors the world over, including Isaias. Suffice it to point to Hungary, Poland, Italy, Turkey and the Philippines, to mention a few examples, and there are others.

But that is a topic for another day. My task now is to proceed covering the subject of the Rule of Law.

II. THE MEANING AND CONSTITUTIONAL SIGNIFICANCE OF THE RULE OF LAW?

1. General Historical Perspective

The Rule of Law, as a "universally applicable principle" is an integral part of human progress—of the legal and spiritual evolution of humanity. One of the achievements of the post World War II period has been the growth and universal acceptance of human rights under the rule of law in all their varied forms. Following in the footsteps of the UN Charter, numerous international resolutions and declarations have been adopted by the UN General Assembly, beginning with the Universal Declaration of Human Rights of 1948, which marks a milestone in the evolution of the international law on human rights. The Declaration has provided the basic framework for the future development of different aspects of human rights and influenced the writing of national constitutions in this respect.

The 1948 Declaration became a universalizing agent, giving legitimacy to the protest movement of all oppressed groups rising in rebellion against unjust systems.

[See paragraph 3 of the Preamble to the Declaration].

This represents a crucial aspect of human progress. The controlling principle of human progress, once gained, tends to become universalized and more or less permanent, despite periodic regression as happened in the Nazi holocaust and as is happening in some places in our time. What is gained becomes part of the common heritage of humankind. Human rights, the rule of law and democracy as the paramount political value of our epoch, reinforce one another, progressively beating down the walls of resistance originating from the forces of tradition or political interests. It is a progress that is continuing, and which will be continually facing challenges of one kind or another.

In terms of the evolution of human rights, a climax was reached in the adoption of the 1966 UN International Covenants on Civil and Political

Rights, and on Economic and Social and Cultural Rights. Article 1 of the Covenant (known as the Common Article) provides: "All peoples have the right to self-determination. By virtue of that right, they freely determine their political status and freely pursue their economic, social and cultural development."

[See the International Covenant on Economic, Social, and Cultural Rights, Dec. 16, 1966, 993 U.N.T.S.3]

In the context of such basic framework of law sanctioned by international agreements, it is important to note that a distinction must be made between a basic legal text like a nation's constitution and the principle of constitutionalism. Constitutionalism is the acceptance of the rule of law by a political community. In a word the rule of law is the soul of a constitutional body.

2. Basic Content of the Rule of Law

A country may have a body of laws, but a body of laws without the rule of law is like a human body without a soul. The same is true with a constitution without constitutionalism. The rule of law is one of the pillars of a constitutional system that provides for the protection of the civil rights and liberties of citizens. The essence of the rule of law is grounded in basic human needs for certainty of rights and protection against arbitrary power. It is thus conceptually opposed to the whims of capricious rulers and, as such, could not have been granted by the good will of kings or princes. Nor did it drop from the sky as a heavenly manna. It is the outcome of millennial struggle waged by suffering humanity, and attained incrementally with enormous sacrifice.

Thus viewed in historical perspective, the rule of law becomes a patrimony of the people. The people obey the law because of their faith in the rule of law. Simply stated, under the rule of law, all persons have equal access to the law. In other words, all are equal in the eyes of the law; and no man is above the law. Put differently, the rule of law creates the condition for obedience of the law which, in turn, ensures peace and stability. Conversely, the absence or non-observance of the rule of law encourages disobedience of the law.

The rule of law should not be seen in isolation; it must be viewed in the context of the totality of a democratic constitutional order. Indeed, there is a critical link between rule of law and democracy; the two concepts are mutually reinforcing in terms of their practical application. For instance, democracy's basic feature as a value system—the equality principle—depends, for its vitality, on the rule of law, principally applied by the courts. When a person's equality rights are violated, there are courts of law to give him relief against the offending party or parties. On the other hand, the rule of law (and the principle of judicial independence on which it depends) relies for its application on general public support, including the unstinting backing of the people's elected representatives.

[*The constitutional principle of an independent judiciary depends on such general public support, a point repeatedly emphasized by the Constitutional Commission of Eritrea, during Eritrea's constitution making process. See below for a brief statement on judicial independence as a condition for the application of the rule of law*]

Just as it took long and hard struggle to establish the primacy of the rule of law in society, it takes constant vigilance to fight against the resort to arbitrariness by rulers who may be tempted to ignore the requirements of the rule of law. In most countries of the world today, issues pertaining to the rule of law and related principles have been addressed under constitutional provisions. Almost all constitutions of the world provide for the rule of law, but there are some instances in which the constitutional provisions are honored more in their breach than in their observance.

The usual excuse given by apologists of regimes that are in breach of the rule of law is the requirements of peace, stability and orderly development. The government, they argue, cannot afford to be weak or to show weakness for the sake of an abstract principle. It cannot be overstressed, however, that real and enduring stability is based on observance of the rule of law. For example, it is claimed by Eritrea's leaders that the work of the special court has had the salutary effect of stemming the tide of corruption. There is no way to prove or disprove this claim. All we know is that the law establishing the special court denies the right of appeal against the decision of the court, a provision which violates the constitution and is contrary to traditionally accepted norms of justice. Even if the claim of controlling corruption is true it should not be allowed to violate the higher values of the rule of law as enshrined in the constitution.

3. Government and the Rule of Law

It bears repetition that the rule of law, or principle of legality, as it is known in European civil law systems, anchors constitutional government. A good government is one that governs according to the law, not according to the whims or caprice of those who are in power. To sum up what has been stated earlier, the underlying principle of the rule of law is simple: it guarantees certainty of rights, equal rights, equal justice under the law, and freedom from arbitrary treatment of citizens. It thus provides the conditions for the obedience of the law and ensures the peace and stability that goes with it.

That is how it works in theory, at least. In practice, governments have been known, throughout history, to ignore the rule of law and establish, or perpetuate, arbitrary rule. It is an important aspect of democratic transition in modern times that arbitrary rule is rare and, where it exists, it is on the defensive. Arbitrary rulers almost always use patriotic terms to justify their rule, reminding one of Samuel Johnson's famous line: *"Patriotism is the last refuge of scoundrels."*

One of the tasks of Parliament will be to guard against any arbitrary acts or tendencies of the Executive branch on any one of its agencies in the conduct of government business. The principles or criteria for judging such acts or tendencies are contained in the Constitution and should be elaborated under laws issued by Parliament. As an Eritrean elder put it at a village meeting during the constitution making process of Eritrea:

"The government needs a strong hand to be able to govern, but it must be harnessed by the *lugam* of the law.

[*During a discussion of the constitutional draft at the village of Ad'Tekelezan, Summer 1996. Lugam means the bridle that guides horses or mules; here it is used as a metaphor for control and accountability*].

The elder's point about the need for strong government is well taken. The Constitutional Commission of Eritrea gave emphasis to the need for a vigorous government and administration but underscored the need for such government to abide by the rule of law, to be accountable and transparent in its work. The primary responsibility for ensuring these safeguards lies with Parliament. Indeed, the Constitution provides for principles or criteria for judging the conduct of the government. The primary institutions charged by the Constitution with the responsibility of monitoring the conduct of government and of censoring arbitrary behavior and breach of law are the Legislature and the Courts of law. Alas! At the moment, there is no constitutionally elected Legislature and the Courts work under debilitating constraint.

[*Anyone who doubts this should ask the now "frozen" President of the Supreme Court of Eritrea who reportedly made a public statement at an international conference regretting the absence of the rule of law in the country.*]

The Challenges Facing Democracy

Winston Churchill famously opined that democracy is the worst form of government, except for all the other forms that have been tried and found wanting.

[*James C. Humes, The Wit and Wisdom of Winston Churchill. 28 (1994)*].

Democracy requires constant vigilance and struggle. In the dynamics of the exercise of governmental power, a country's leadership has the responsibility to offer a vision and define policies and programs to actualize such vision. When engaged in such exercise in a democratic context, or when following democratic procedures, a leadership may face problems or constraints. In short, it may face seemingly insuperable challenges. It is the task of lawyers and political scientists and of all concerned citizens to monitor and evaluate the manner in which a leadership responds to such challenges. **It is the business of Parliament to do so on a daily basis**.

When a challenge becomes acute, it might be tempting for a leadership to follow the line of least resistance—to suspend democratic procedures and impose emergency measures in the name of national unity and stability. To void such occurrence, the constitution provides for the type of situation when a state of emergency may be declared with the approval of Parliament.

[See Erit. Cosnt. Art 27].

III. Judicial Independence and The Rule of Law

As already noted, the principle of an independent judiciary is the keystone of the constitutional edifice, particularly as it pertains to the "Bill of Rights." A judiciary that is insulated from the pressures of powerful interests in society, and that can render justice without fear or favor, acts as the best guarantee for people to live and go about their business with a sense of security and trust in the rule of law. In that sense, therefore, the rule of law and its custodian in the form of an independent judiciary is the foundation of peace and orderly development.

This is connected to the fundamental right of equality under the law, which is, as noted before, a cardinal constitutional, democratic principle. In this conception of the law, it is regarded as a neutral force, above all taint of class or clan, party or personal predilection.

But since such a lofty and impersonal conception of law, it cannot apply itself, it demands institutions and mechanisms for its application. That is the job cut out for an independent judiciary functioning in the administration of justice. Judgeship is a noble calling requiring special qualities. It calls for rare intellect and character, especially in the case of those sitting at the highest court of a country, such as the Supreme Court or Constitutional Court.

In Eritrea, the question of judicial independence and the role of the judiciary was repeatedly raised during the constitutional debates. How is judicial independence secured in actual practice? The answer lies, first and foremost, in the culture of the society—in its felt need to be aware of and support the principle of judicial independence—from the ordinary citizen to the highest ranks of political leadership. There must be a national consensus that independence of the judiciary benefits everybody and deserves the support of everybody, irrespective of political views, ethnic or class background. And the second answer is that such consensus must have institutional expression, which is why we have or must have a Judicial Service Commission that is responsible for the recruitment of judges and for determining the terms and conditions of their service, including their progress within such service.

[see Chapter Eleven of the Constitution of Eritrea, especially Articles 48, 49, 52 and 53].

IV. THE WAY FORWARD

As we contemplate the Fate of Eritrea in these troubled times with a President trashing the constitution and even threatening to do away with the sovereignty of the country, let us consider the following:

1. **First and foremost**, Eritreans need to be clear about one thing, whatever their differences in other respects—they must insist on the implementation of their constitution. The constitution is their common property and the ultimate guarantee for the protection of their rights and interests. The government's promise to hold general elections in late 2001 was considered a hopeful beginning. But promises have been made and easily

broken in the past, including the undertaking to put the constitution into effect soon after its ratification.

The Constitutional Commission of Eritrea opted not to include an article in the constitution mentioning a date for its coming into effect on the strength of such implicit understanding. In retrospect, some thought it was a mistake not to fix a due date for which the Commission, and I personally as its chairman, take responsibility. It was a decision based on trust. There is a commercial ad of an insurance company showing the picture of a little child touching the base of the horn of a rhinoceros. The caption reads *"Trust is not being afraid even if you're vulnerable."* The Commission chose not to be afraid, even though it was vulnerable to betrayal. It made a decision based on trust, and has been living the consequences.

In retrospect and in view of the suppression of the constitution by "President" Isaias Afwerki, it makes no difference whether a due date is included or not in the constitution.

2. **Second**, we must insist on national unity while pushing for democratic transition on the basis of our constitution. In 2001, the announcement by the chairman of the committee that drafted the law on political parties that it has completed its work was heartening news. The appearance of more than one party, though not necessarily a panacea, should not be seen as leading to division; that myth has been exploded. Our people have not fought a thirty-year war only to tear their country apart. To believe and insist otherwise is to hold the Eritrean public in contempt. If there appear elements that preach division let them be judged in the court of public opinion and calmly rejected with patience and resolve, and perhaps with a modicum of pity. To quote an American sage:"*...If there be any among us who wish to destroy the union, or to change its republican form, let them stand undisturbed, as monuments of the safety with which error of opinion may be tolerated where reason is left free to combat it.*"

[Thomas Jefferson, Inaugural Address, 1801.]

3. **Third**, we must insist on reconciliation of the fractured parts of our political body politic. National unity does not mean only organizational unity of the governing party—whichever party is governing—but unity across factional lines. One of the issues that the authors of the Berlin letter raised for "President" Isaias' serious consideration concerns national reconciliation. The letter urged a call for reconciliation "extended to all Eritreans irrespective of belief or political affiliation to join hands in rebuilding a shattered society and economy." The letter further urges the leadership of the governing party to provide political space for groups or individuals and thus cure the sense of alienation experienced by segments of our society. Such a political space is required by the constitution in no uncertain terms.

There have been complaints by some that the constitution does not provide for the formation of political parties. This is wrong and the establishment and work of the parliamentary committee that completed its task of drafting the law respecting political parties proved them wrong. Some have also pointed to defects of the constitution on various grounds, including the fact that it was drafted by members of the EPLF and is, for that reason, suspect! Some have even accused me of being disingenuous for being critical of some of Isaias' policies and style of leadership as if I didn't collaborate with him as a member of his party. This kind of accusation is in part a function of the factional strife—ELF v. EPLF, etc.—which has been an unfortunate aspect of modern Eritrean history. It is also, in a few instances, partly the work of people who satisfy their egos by indulging in slanderous attacks. I choose to ignore such attacks. But I want to clear a couple of points with respect to the making of the Eritrean constitution.

First of all, there is no such thing as a perfect constitution; constitutions are human-made, and humans are not perfect. But the three years of process-driven constitution making of Eritrea has been hailed as the way to go by international observers.

[That was indeed one reason why an international organization recommended me to act as consultant to the Nigerian government in their on-going constitutional review. This honor belongs to Eritrea.]

Despite our best efforts, however, there is bound to be imperfection, and such defects as may be found in the constitution can be corrected in time as the constitution is put into effect. The Eritrean constitution contains all the central principles essential for the proper functioning of government and a healthy relationship between government and citizens, including a Bill of Rights, an independent judiciary, term limits for the president as well as appropriate mechanisms for governmental accountability. The proof of the pudding is in the eating. Let us work towards its implementation and see how it works.

As for the fact that it is the work of members of the EPLF, I'll repeat what I said to many during public meetings among Eritreans in the Diaspora. Any government has the right to form commissions to draft a constitution. The EPLF government legitimately formed the Eritrean Constitutional Commission and most of the members of the Commission, including myself were members of the EPLF. The real question was: Did the Commission, once appointed, work with autonomy and did it discharge its responsibilities properly? The answer to both questions is a resounding yes. It is now time to go beyond this issue and insist on the implementation of our constitution so that the people can begin to enjoy their rights and the government act according to the requirements of the constitution. There is no better subject around which people can rally than their common property. And whatever defects the ratified constitution may have can be addressed by an amendment in accordance with the provisions of the constitution.

4. **Fourth**, there must be a strict separation of party and government, and PFDJ must make full accounting of its economic activities. A special Commission of Inquiry must be established to investigate its assets and liabilities. The issue of restitution of assets that should appropriately belong to the government should be made and such restitution contemplated

before the election is held, with a view to creating a level playing field in which PFDJ does not enjoy a disproportionate financial advantage over other parties. This is not the first time that I am advocating government appropriation of PFDJ's assets. I expressed the same opinion at a public meeting in 1994, at the start of the constitution making process, in response to a question by a member of the audience.

I said above that the rule of law and democracy are mutually reinforcing concepts. This point cannot be overstressed. It is necessary to appreciate the relationship of the two. I have unabashedly preached the gospel of constitutionalism and the rule of law as the crown jewel of constitutional democracy. I recognize the interdependence of the two—the rule of law depends on a democratic order, and a democratic order fares better under multi-party, rather than under a one-party system. Accordingly, I am reiterating my commitment to multi-party democracy. A tantalizingly promising beginning had been made in the form of the draft law on political parties, before Isaias locked up the main actors in that promising exercise.

[Indeed, the man who chaired that committee, Mahmud Sherifo died in prison and others are wasting in the same prison].

The public needs to be continually engaged in debating the subject of multi-party democracy for which Sherifo and his fellow prisoners gave their lives, as well as for the implementation of the constitution.

Let us all hope that the common good will be the guiding principle in all our deliberations.

* * *

N.B.

This paper was written in the context of extraordinary historic events occurring and producing their own momentum. Such events are occurring under the ongoing non-transparent "negotiations" being

undertaken by a dictator on the side of Eritrea, and by an elected Prime Minster on Ethiopia's side.

However, the tragic fact of a runaway President betraying his trust should not affect the validity of the points raised in the paper which proceeds on the assumption that, although illegally suppressed, Eritrea does have a duly written and ratified constitution, which will be implemented sooner or later, following regime change.

DEMOCRACY AND THE ROLE OF PARLIAMENT UNDER THE ERITREAN CONSTITUTION

I. Introduction

Eritrea's constitutional moment stretched out for three years from April 1994 to May 1997. By constitutional moment, I mean the meeting point between a nation's past, present and future, the time when all the principal constitutional issues are--or should be--confronted and debated: the basic principles of governance, the rights and duties of citizens, and the powers and responsibilities of government.

The Eritrean experience of constitution making was marked by large-scale and intense participation of the public in village and town meetings at which most of the main issues were raised and debated. Of the issues raised by the public, such as the type of government structure, electoral system, decentralization, political pluralism, religion and the state, etc., none was more widely debated than the question of government power and how it impinges on the rights of the people. The problem of power and how different societies, at different times, have dealt with it is always a fascinating subject to contemplate; it becomes a crucial matter when one is engaged in creating the Constitution by which such power will be regulated. In the Eritrean case, the people were not only fascinated by the process that engaged their intellectual resources, but followed the process, with great interest, every step of the way until the Constitution was ratified on May 23, 1997.

The focus of the present paper will be the role of Parliament in a democratic system of government, under the Eritrean Constitution. The paper is based on a chapter of a book that I am writing on Eritrea's constitution making process and commentaries on the text of the Constitution which is nearing completion. I chose this topic for a special publication of the North Carolina Review of Law and Commercial Regulation because the Parliament under the Eritrean Constitution is conceived as a critical institution, designed to ensure the healthy political development of the new nation. My colleagues at the Constitutional Commission of Eritrea and I laid particular emphasis on this point throughout the constitution making process and I dwelt on it also in my final address to the concluding session of the Council of the Commission.

Following the Introduction, the paper discusses the role of Parliament in relation to the concept of democracy in historical perspective. This is followed by a discussion on electoral systems in general, and the next section deals with the role of Parliament and parliamentary process under the Eritrean Constitution. A concluding section sums up Eritrea's approach to democratic transition in the context of global development trends.

In what remains of this introductory section, and in anticipation of more detailed discussions in later sections, I will offer a brief review of the current discourse on democracy and its relation to constitutional government and electoral politics.

In the on-going debate on the definition of democracy, the concept of poliarchy put forward by Robert Dahl offers a useful variation on the theme of democratic pluralism, underscoring the importance of freedom of speech and press for meaningful pluralist politics. Without these "civil freedoms" people may not be able to express their political preferences in a meaningful way. [See Robert Dahl, Poliarchy: Participation and Opposition (New Haven: Yale University Press, 1971.)] Others have elaborated on this theme leading to a minimalist conception of democracy, focussing on election of representatives as the critical requirement. This minimalist conception stresses the need for minimal levels of "civil freedom" so that electoral politics--competition and popular participation-- can be meaningful. [Cf. Larry Diamond, Is the Third Wave Over? Journal of Democracy, July 1996, pp. 20-37.]

That democratic government, be it parliamentary or presidential, requires popular participation and competition is beyond dispute. What has been termed electoral democracy is, therefore, a crucial component of democratic government. Does this minimalist conception embrace other critical requirements for a meaningful democratic government? Does parliamentary government *per se* a democracy make?

A proper answer to this question must begin by stating that Parliament, as a representative institution, by whatever name it is known, is the primary national institution accountable to the citizens of a country. It is, in theory, the principal mediator in the dialectic of the governors and the governed. There is an inherent tension in that dialectic even in the best of circumstances, and the citizens' representatives are--or should be--the first line of defense for the protection of the rights of their constituents. Democracy and electoral politics are thus critically linked to the role of Parliament in a constitutional order. We shall see the historical and theoretical origin of that link in the next section.

In answering the question posed above, whether parliamentary or electoral politics, per se, meets all the requirements of democracy, it must be borne in mind that constitutional government, or any government, does not function in a vacuum. The overall historical context--the economic condition, the social milieu and cultural heritage of the country, as well as the political environment--combine to influence the outcome of the democratic process. Moreover, there is the role of leadership; in the dynamic interaction of principle and practice, in any historical context, the role of leadership is critical. A wise and able leadership (wisdom and ability do not always come together) looks beyond temporary advantages, into the future. A wise leadership endeavors to instill and maintain respect for the law--for a government of law, as against a "government of men."

During the extensive public consultation of Eritrea's constitution making process of 1994-1997, these points--leadership and the imperative of a government of law--were among the most frequently raised and debated. The principal concerns of most people expressed during those debates may be summed up in three sets of issues: (1) government accountability and transparency, (2) the need for multi-parties to secure accountability and transparency, and (3) economic policy and social justice. The first two sets of issues are in line with the current conception of democracy and constitutional government, and they have been answered by Eritrea's Constitution under which they are guaranteed. The third set of issues is not covered under the current conception of democracy. This conception, therefore, falls short of being complete and as such cannot be used as the sole criterion for judging the democratic record of a country.

With respect to the third issue--economic policy and social justice--the governing party of the country, the People's Front for Democracy and Justice (PFDJ), considers rapid economic growth and the consequent of the standard of living of the greater mass of the population as an overriding priority. It expressed serious doubts as to whether a multi-party system would work at the present. The party is fearful that multi-party system might adversely affect the priority goal of rapid growth as well as the stability required for such growth and for good governance in general. The implication is that it may be quite a while before the country will have multi-parties, and that Parliament would be composed of members of the governing party only, or predominantly, for the foreseeable future.

Given Eritrea's historical circumstances, the logic of PFDJ's policy of rapid economic growth as a priority seemed to be irresistible. But even if one accepts the premise of the policy and the contention that multi-parties in the short-run would be contrary to rapid economic growth and prosperity, one would, nonetheless, need to make a quantum leap of faith that a one-party regime will bring about prosperity and an improvement in people's standard of living. In this respect, it is hard to ignore the cautionary tales of the corruption and waste of African one-party regimes of the past thirty years. Most of them started out with promises of future prosperity, based on the false assumption that a short-term sacrifice--an exchange, so to speak, of Bread for Liberty-- would eventually pay ample dividends, in terms of economic prosperity and social progress. But Bread and Liberty are not, and should never be, mutually exclusive, and democracy and development should go hand in hand. In any case, in the Eritrean case, the short-term proved to be too long and the promised goods were not delivered.

The Problematic of Democracy and Development.

The better approach to this subject is to think of democratic politics and development in dynamic terms, as a sort of work in progress, rather than as a settled matter, fixed in a time warp. This is not to say that there are no fundamental principles governing the subject; there are, and we will make an attempt to state and place in historical perspective such principles, in the section that follows. However, it cannot be overstressed that, in addition to commitment to principles, mechanisms of control should be put in place and their operation watched with vigilance in order to hold governments accountable. A vigorous Parliament is one such mechanism, as was noted before. But what if the members of Parliament all belong and are beholden to the party in power because there are no other contending parties? Are there other effective mechanisms that can make up for the absence of a parliamentary check on governmental power? Different countries may provide different answers to this question. But one thing is certain, traditional representative institutions cannot effectively perform the required function of control.

Which leaves us with one choice: whatever the circumstances that may extenuate the postponement of multi-parties, **there must be a time frame within which a one party-system must give way to multi-parties**.

II. Parliament and the Democratic Idea

Ours is the age of democracy. Only a few extremists now dispute the fact that democracy is the most desirable political system; even autocratic rulers pay lip service to it. It has taken over two hundred years of philosophical discourse and political struggle for the democratic idea to gain universal acceptance and reign supreme. But as Alexis de Tocqueville has noted, it is a malleable concept subject to different interpretations to advance different ends. Commenting on the relationship between democracy and popular sovereignty, de Tocqueville notes that democracy constitutes the social state, "a way of being for society", whereas popular sovereignty constitutes political right, a form of government.

From the philosophical discourse of revolutionary France (1789-1794) to the first half of the 19th century, two basic elements emerged to define democracy's essential content which have been characterized as "political" and "sociological." But even de Tocqueville qualifies his own dichotomy by saying that popular sovereignty and democracy are correlative terms: the one presents the theoretical idea, while the other presents its practical realization. It took the authoritative works of Montesquieu's *Esprit de Lois*, and Rousseau's *Contrat Social* to rescue the idea of democracy from its association with the archaic, and to advance it to represent the twin principles of self-government and legitimacy. Montesquieu the uncontested authority, and one of the sources of inspiration for the American constitution makers, places legislative power squarely on the shoulders of the people's representatives.

Great thinkers like Montesquieu and Rousseau thought of democracy as an ideal type that would work "if there were a people of gods," as Rousseau put it. The historical significance of their writings lies in the revolutionary implication of the idea of democracy. The idea of democracy eventually yielded to that of popular sovereignty--Rousseau's "general will". Popular sovereignty, in turn, yielded to representative government. The great revolution of modern times lies in the process of institution building from the popular base. It was revolutionary in that it implied, and eventually led to, the destruction of *the ancien regime*--the feudal order--and its replacement by elected representatives.

This leads us to the practical application of the idea of democracy, or what we may call the problematic of democracy. Earlier writers, including the 18th century French philosophers, criticized democracy as a method of government. The main criticism was that it leads to instability and consequent abuse of its principles. The French Encyclopidists denounced it in those terms.

In England, the Revolution of 1688 had already instituted a measure of representative government, albeit qualified by the fact that the House of Commons embraced, at the time, only the landed gentry. John Locke's Second Treatise, which puts property ownership at the center of political rights, was the gospel of England's ascendant class of property owners and was a major source of inspiration of the American Revolution, of the Declaration of Independence of 1776 and the Constitution of 1789. Paradoxically, the ideas that were born in Europe exerted their influence on the American revolutionaries and constitution makers, and then made a Trans-Atlantic journey back from the newly formed United States of America back to revolutionary France to reinforce the democratic idea of government. The celebrated French constitutionalist, the Abbe Sieyes, clearly articulated the principles of representative government. He wrote: "there are two ways of bringing the citizen together for the purpose of making law directly: the citizens may exercise their rights to make laws directly, or they may entrust it <u>to representatives, who are much more capable than the citizen of knowing the general interest."</u> [7.Note the underlined words. Knowledge of relevant issues and ability to properly represent the constituent in articulating them is a major reason why there should be representatives apart from the practical considerations such as distance, etc. ...]

Representative government as an expression of democracy became irresistible in modern nation states; in the context of a given country's size--larger than the city-states of ancient Athens, or the traditional village community--and eventually also the technicalities that must be mastered in a more complex polity, representative government seemed to be the only alternative. The resurgence of democracy in the post-industrial revolution period was connected with a phase of political struggle in which people played a central part. Democracy and representative government, hitherto viewed as technically distinct, now became one in tracing power to a popular base, both resting on people's sovereignty.

In the Constitution of Eritrea, the principles of democracy and people's sovereignty is clearly defined. Article 1(5) of the Constitution provides that in the State of Eritrea, "supreme power is vested in the people, and shall be exercised pursuant to the provisions of this constitution." And the equal participation of citizens "in all areas of human endeavor" is guaranteed under Article 7, which charges the State to create conditions necessary for developing a democratic culture defined by free and critical thinking, tolerance and national consensus.

It bears reiterating that representative democracy is a more complex form of self-government by the people in contrast to the more direct form of self-government that is associated with the Athenian *polis or with village democracy in much of African societies.* The modern State brought different communities together thus making representative government an imperative. This fact necessitated the adoption of mechanisms of electing people's representatives at the national level, in accordance with the requirements of the times. Hence the significance of electoral systems.

III. Democracy and Electoral Systems

An Electoral System constitutes the meeting point between popular sovereignty and representative government. It deals with how the citizens' voting rights--the primary expression of their sovereignty-- are translated into parliamentary seats. In these parliamentary seats resides legislative power with its associated power of control of the purse and of monitoring the executive power. The electoral system is the most fundamental element of representative democracy.

Elections express the principle of government by the consent of the governed and should, therefore, be designed and organized in a way that would enable the governed to choose the best available candidate to represent them. An Electoral System must be designed, in other words, in such a way as to enable every citizen to participate freely and fully in the election of representatives. The Constitutional Commission of Eritrea included, in its Issues Papers a study of this subject and identified four general purposes that must be served by elections:

1. reflection of the main opinions of the electorate;
2. establishment of majority rule;
3. election of suitable representatives; and
4. Formation of robust and stable government.

Implicit in these general purposes is another feature of elections, i.e. that the elections should take place at regular intervals and for specified terms of office. In the case of Eritrea, the term of office of five years has been specified in the Constitution, [Art 31(5)], whereas details on the time of elections together with other details, is left to be specified by legislation on electoral laws. The fixed term of office, or mandate, enables citizens to review the performance of their elected representatives and to pass judgement at the next election either by re-electing them or terminating their mandate and choosing other candidates. Election time has thus juridical as well as political significance: For electors and candidates alike, it is a day of judgement on which the quality of representative government depends.

Electoral Systems

There are different types of electoral systems whose variety reflects national political and demographic factors. Most typically, however, they may be divided into two broad categories: the majority system and the proportional representation (PR) system.

<u>Majority System:</u> This system, also known as "first-past-the-post" is one in which one person is elected by a relative majority: that is to say, the person obtaining the most votes, from among competing candidates, is declared elected. Experience in many countries over the years has shown that this system failed to fulfill the purposes listed above, particularly in terms of reflecting the views or interests of the majority of the electing citizens. The following examples of voting results of four candidates participating in an election under this system illustrated the failure of the system in terms of reflecting the majority of electors:

Candidates Votes Obtained

A 7,000
B 4,000
C 3,500
D 2,500

The failure of the majority voting system to represent majority views is demonstrated in this example, in that candidate A would be declared elected with a 7, 000 vote, whereas the combined vote for candidates B, C and D is 10,000. Given a second chance, it is conceivable that the voters might prefer candidate B or C.

A study of the election history of several countries shows that attempts were made to remedy this inherent weakness of the system. One solution is to provide for second ballot, or more, in order to give people an opportunity to re-cast their votes in favor of one or the other of the candidates who received fewer votes on the first count. The most frequent practice has been to have the two candidates with most votes to submit to a second ballot. This and similar attempts at modifying the majority system imply financial cost and voter fatigue. The alternative is Proportional Representation.

Proportional Representation: For a number of years now, proportional representation (PR) has been advanced as a better electoral formula, particularly for countries with multi-ethnic composition which is the case in most countries in Africa. The principal argument in favor of PR is that it protects minorities or facilitates the representation of their voice in national politics. There have been some instructive lessons drawn from studies conducted recently on Southern African elections which demonstrate the superiority of PR.

The comparative advantage of PR over the majority system should be analyzed in relation to party politics. The primary consideration is that parties should obtain seats in the Parliament in proportion to their support in the electorate which is possible under PR more than under the majority system. The simplest arrangement is one in which the number of seats in a constituency is divided into the total votes cast in an election, so that each party obtains its share of seats in relation to the votes it obtains at the polls. For example, in a constituency where 150,000 votes are cast and the constituency is entitled to five seats in Parliament, each party will be entitled to one seat for every 30,000 vote it gets at the poll.

Different varieties of this formula have been used in attempts to have a more equitable representation. Opinions differ as to the value of PR, some even arguing that it is not suitable to "agrarian" societies. The principal criticism of PR is that it weakens the link between the individual members of Parliament and their constituencies. This prevents the development of what has been called the "vertical" dimension of democracy (i.e. the representational relationship between political elites and the "ordinary people" with a common political interest) and reduces the prospects for the consolidation of democratic rule.

These arguments, among others, will no doubt be considered and weighed carefully at the time when the Eritrean Parliament debates the

Bill on the electoral laws stipulated in Article 31(6). of the Constitution. The Committee on electoral law had started its work when the war broke out between Ethiopia and Eritrea, and the Eritrean President dissolved it along with the Committee on Parties.[**Twenty years later, the Constitution remains unimplemented. Hence the on-going protest and demand for change**]

The Constitutional Commission left the matter of choosing the type of electoral system to be determined by legislation. It nonetheless debated the issue at length. In the course of the debate, it was pointed out that PR assumes the existence of several parties which is not the case in Eritrea at the moment. Future legislation can adjust the rules to reflect changing needs and demands, including the need to enable small Parties proper representation. In this respect, the question of ethnic minorities is relevant. In the event that the future legislation on political parties prohibits the formation of political parties on religious and ethnic basis, as it is likely to do, ensuring equitable ethnic representation becomes a relevant issue. In the Eritrean context, the governing party, starting from its formation in the early 1970's, practiced an inclusive national politics in which all the ethnic groups were encouraged to join and did join. This policy, which represented the imperative of a national liberation struggle, continued after independence as one of the supposedly basic principles of the Front (PFDJ), as speeches of the Eritrean President, as chairman of the PFDJ indicated. [Cf. President Isaias' speech to the first Party Conference in late August 1995 where he laid emphasis to the need to deepen and maintain the national, as against parochial consciousness.]

In the future deliberations of the Parliament the principal objective should be fair and equitable representation of the whole population in the nation's legislative body. As already mentioned, the Constitutional Commission's Proposals state that whatever the system chosen, it must be capable of ensuring fair and adequate representation of the whole population. It bears repetition that, since electoral systems may be changed from time to time to suit the demands of changing circumstances, a provision on electoral systems should be left out of the Constitution to be dealt with by legislation. [this was the recommendation in the Commission's Proposal...Accordingly, Article 30(2) provides that the National Assembly shall enact an electoral law, which shall ensure the representation and participation of the Eritrean people."]

The Electoral Commission

The Constitution provides for the establishment of an Electoral Commission. [Article 58]. The Constitution is fastidious about the operational independence of the Electoral Commission because the integrity of the electoral process must be maintained scrupulously. It provides that the said Commission must operate independently, without any interference, in order to ensure that free and fair elections are held. The Election Commission is empowered to manage the implementation of the elections, decide on issues raised in the course of the electoral process, and formulate and implement civic educational programs relating to elections and other democratic procedures. [NB. (1) Electoral Commissioners are appointed by the President with the approval of the National Assembly. (Article 58(2); (2) The details on the powers and duties and organization of electoral commission is left to de determined by a law to be enacted by the National Assembly (Article 58(3).]

IV. COMPOSITION AND FUNCTION OF ERITREA'S PARLIAMENT

Composition

The Eritrean Parliament consists of a single Chamber National Assembly. It is composed of representatives of the people elected by direct and secret ballot by all citizens who are qualified to vote. [31(3)] Any Eritrean citizen, 18 years of age or more, has the right to vote. The qualifications and election of members of Parliament and the conditions for vacating their seats are determined by legislation issued by Parliament.

Members of Parliament (MPs), though elected from particular electoral districts, are representatives of the Eritrean people as a whole. In discharging their duties as MPs, they are governed by the objectives and principles of the Constitution, the interest of the people and the country and their conscience. [31(4)

Parliamentary mandate lasts for a term of five years from the day of the first session held, following a general election. Exceptionally, where there exists a state of war, or a state of emergency in terms of article 26 of the Constitution, which would prevent a normal election from being held, Parliament may, by a resolution supported by not less than two-thirds vote of all its members, extend its term for a period not exceeding six months. [Actually, since the President suppressed for twenty years, all this just an academic exercise, albeit an instructive one.]

Three topics at least, need elaboration, out of the foregoing discussion:

Single-Chamber nature of the Eritrean Parliament;
Universal, direct and secret voting (suffrage)
The national character of the MP's duties.

Single Chamber Assembly

What were the reasons that led Eritrean constitution-makers to choose a single Chamber Parliament, in preference over a two-Chamber Parliament? The question was a part of the 23 issues that the Constitutional Commission grappled with at the start of its work and was, accordingly, a subject of research. The team that researched the subject submitted a report with a divided opinion: a majority proposing a one-Chamber Parliament, and a minority view arguing in favor of two-Chamber Parliament.

The arguments advanced in support of a two-Chamber Parliament outlined three principal advantages: (a) it ensures wider representation of a nation, especially one with a multi-ethnic composition; (b) it can guarantee the issuing of better laws and policies, because it ensures more deliberation and ampler time-frame. (c) it can help in the resolution of tension that may arise out of controversies between the Executive and Legislative branches. The proponents of this minority view recognized two drawbacks of a two-Chamber Parliament, i.e. that it may involve delay and expenses, but nonetheless cogently argued that these disadvantages are outweighed by the benefits.

The majority view argued: (a) that a single-Chamber Parliament better reflects the sovereignty of the people and enacts laws without undue concern over the special interests in society, be they based on ethnicity or class; (b) it is speedy; and (c) it is less costly. The supporters of the majority view were aware of the drawbacks of potential haste and tension that may arise between the Executive and Legislative branches, but argued that the advantages out-weigh the drawbacks, and that constitutional provisions can be devised to overcome them. For a nation like Eritrea, a dynamic leadership is needed, one that reflects unified representation of the people in one Chamber, even in the context of a (future) multi-party system. Whatever merit the two-Chamber system may have in other situations, the historical and socio-political circumstances of Eritrea is such that there is no need to constitutionalize divisions that have been resolved particularly due to the recent history of a 30-year armed struggle against a common enemy. The "objective" conditions of a country must determine the type of system constitution-makers adopt.

The Commission accepted these arguments and decided to adopt a one-Chamber Parliament. In making such a choice, the Commission added a further point: whatever groups in society might have merited representation in a second Chamber, can be accommodated through the careful drawing up of electoral laws and procedures. In this respect, the Commission considered, but ultimately rejected, the practice followed in some countries under which the head of State appoints to the Parliament members of certain groups in society, such as elders or chieftains, or professional people. In the considered opinion of the Commission, such people can and should be encouraged to enter Parliament through the electoral process.

Universal Suffrage

A detailed discussion of this topic is not necessary beyond stressing its constitutional significance as a keystone in the edifice of parliamentary democracy. Voting must be universal, i.e. every adult citizen qualified to vote has the right to participate in voting; the voting must be secret, and the voter must be able to vote directly, not through third parties.

Universal adult suffrage is an electoral category which historically marks the triumph of the right of common people against the prior system of suffrage that had been limited to the privileged classes. In England, known as the home of modern parliamentary government, this right was not won until the Reform Act of 1832 was passed by the British Parliament, and even then, it was limited by the requirements of property ownership, a requirement that took several decades to be eliminated. Moreover, it took a long, drawn-out battle of the suffragette movement in England until the 1920's before the vote could be extended to women in England, and until the 1960's in some countries in Europe, like Switzerland.

The requirement of direct voting is to be distinguished from indirect vote. Indirect vote is vote that is exercised indirectly through community or clan leaders, or through elected members of local assemblies. In other words, citizens do not elect their representatives directly themselves. This is a rare political phenomenon nowadays. Then there is the secrecy principle that ensures that the elector casts his vote in an enclosed space out of sight of anybody. This is also obviously an essential requirement designed to enable the voter to exercise his right without fear or pressure of any kind. The electoral law must make provisions to facilitate this and other requirements to ensure a free and fair election.

The practice of having election observers to witness the electoral process helps guarantee free and fair elections.

Members of Parliament are required by the Constitution to discharge their duties by thinking of themselves first and foremost as representatives of the whole nation. This does not mean that they forget all about their constituencies; on the contrary, they must also represent the views and interests of their constituents and maintain regular contact with them. Article Eritrean people as a whole. In discharging their duties, they are governed by the objectives and principles of the Constitution, the interests of the people and the country and their conscience."

Powers and Duties of Parliament

The members of the National assembly collectively constitute the Legislature. Following their election, and by virtue of the elections, the representatives of the people are collectively associated with government authority. In terms of the Constitution of Eritrea, the members of the Legislature who are elected directly by the people, collectively embody the democratic idea of representative government, as was noted previously. In what follows, we will explore in what way this democratic idea is to be translated into legislative power.

The power of the Legislature may be divided into four main categories: (a) legislation, *strictu sensu*, (b) oversight of executive or administrative matters. (c) hearing citizen complaints, and (d) approval of appointments.

(a) Legislation

To begin with, the National Assembly must be bound by the principles enumerated in the Constitution and is by duty bound to strive to fulfil the objectives stated therein. And according to the Constitution, it has the power "to enact laws and pass resolutions for the peace, stability, development and social justice of Eritrea." [32(1)(a)] Only Parliament (the National Assembly) is the sole legislative authority of the State and any matters that is legislative in nature (law) must come out of Parliament or by delegation from Parliament.((32(b) Such delegation must itself come under the authority of law passed by Parliament. The Constitution puts it this way: "Unless authorized by a law, no person or organization shall have the power to make decisions having the force of law." [32(b)]

This being the principle, it must be noted, nonetheless, that the Executive branch of government impinges on the legislative power of Parliament in two respects. First, it has the power of initiative and the near-monopoly expertise in researching and preparing the draft bill which it then presents to Parliament for its deliberation and enactment. Even in countries with immense resources, like the United States of America, where Congress commands a good deal of human and financial resources to conduct its own research and prepare draft laws, the comparatively greater resource at the command of the Executive branch gives it greater advantage in this respect. In countries like Eritrea, there is an overwhelming advantage in favor of the Executive branch.

In theory, however, in terms of constitutional principle--Parliament can reject all drafts prepared by the Executive. In practice this occurs rarely for political and pragmatic reasons of national interest. A government in a parliamentary system enjoys a majority of votes in Parliament on which it can rely to ensure the passage of draft laws that it submits. Can the government of a party in power always rely on its members? The answer is that it almost always can, but that in some instances, members may "vote their conscience", as the saying goes. This may occur in matters involving moral issues such as capital punishment, abortion or other questions concerning human rights. The experience of other parliamentary systems shows that the party whips (who enforce party discipline in Parliament) normally release their members from their obligation to "toe the line."

In presidential systems like the United States, the doctrine of Separation of Powers holds sway to a great extent. Even though there re party whips in Congress, there is less strict control over party loyalty and respect for the President The leader of the party) and his power of persuasion may cause party alignment over nearly all issues. If a member insists in "voting his conscience" greater pressure may be exerted or some bargaining may be struck, including promises of satisfying some demands of the particular member, in respect of favors done for his constituency. Votes may then be obtained in exchange for particular favors, which is in the nature of the give-and-take of politics.

The other area in which Executive power impinges on the Legislature is delegated legislation. In almost all major legislation, the laws passed by Parliament contain "an enabling clause" under which Parliament delegates its legislative authority to a Minister or another member of the Executive. In the hierarchy of laws of a country, starting with the Constitution, the higher law contains basic principles or major policy issues which lay down the framework of powers and duties or rights and obligations. The lower down we go in the hierarchy the more detailed the provisions become, from the minute details on organization of municipal government, for example, to the circulars or guidelines that a minister issues for his employees to follow.

In the Constitution of Eritrea, the work of legislation under which only Parliament has authority include the following:

- Approval of the national budget and enactment of tax law. [32(3)]
- Ratification, by law, of international agreements. [32(4)
- Authorization of the government to borrow money "pursuant to law." [32(5)
- Approval of state of war or peace or national emergency. [32(6)]

As stated above, there is an "omnibus" clause which gives power to Parliament to pass laws or resolutions "for the peace, stability, etc… of Eritrea" [Article 31(1). Theoretically, Parliament can take initiative, or cause initiative to be taken, to research, study and pass laws concerning the matters of national stability, development and good governance. Almost any subject can be covered by these topics. In practice, of course, it will be the Executive branch of the government which will take the initiative, as already noted.

(b) (c): Parliamentary Oversight and Audience of Citizens' Complaints.

Article 32(7) of the Constitution gives power to Parliament "to oversee the execution of Laws," and discharge its oversight authority…to enact such laws and to establish such standing and ad hoc committees as it deems necessary."[32(12)]

The power of Parliament to oversee the work of the Executive rests on the principle of popular sovereignty which Parliament represents by virtue of its election by the people. The electoral process involves, as we saw, investiture of legislative authority collectively on those who are elected to represent the people. It also involves a legitimizing process under which the voting public transfers to Parliament based on its (voting public's) sovereignty. This legitimation extends to the initiation, monitoring and control of government policy.

There is thus an organic link between the various categories under which Parliament seeks to exercise its power. Hence the combined treatment of the two topics of (a) and (b) under this sub-section of the paper. The initial impetus that sets the machinery of inquiry, monitoring or control may come from an individual member of Parliament or a committee of Parliament, or it may be based on the complaints of citizens either as affected individuals or groups, or as concerned subjects. This process, and the parliamentary authority on which it is based, makes for a healthy interaction between government and citizens. Through its power of oversight, normally exercised through parliamentary committees, the Legislature activates the principle of government accountability thus accomplishing two basic, and related purposes: keeping the members of the Executive branch "on leash" and addressing citizens' grievances.

How this task is performed is a question related to the matter of parliamentary process which will be discussed in the next section. But we should note here that there are several ways in which citizens' grievances may be aired and addressed. There may be a variety of public forums organized in pursuance of the citizens' rights of freedom of association, opinion and conscience, notably the right to use the Press and other Media to those ends. Practices develop which may become constitutional conventions under which rights are exercised balanced by responsibilities. It takes time before such conventions become accepted part of the constitutional process, and the parliamentary immunity of members of the Legislature plays a crucial role in the development, nurturing and maintenance of such conventions which gives life and force to the text of the constitution.

(d). Approval of Appointments

The power of appointment is one of the powers reserved to the Executive branch, notably to the President. But there are certain offices of the state which are regarded as so important that the appointment of people who fill them are made to be subject to parliamentary approval. The Constitution of Eritrea has singled out the following office holders to be subject to such parliamentary approval, all under Article 42(7):

All ministers;
All Commissioners;
Auditor-General;
Head of the Bank of Eritrea (Governor);
Chief Justice, and Justices of the Supreme Court.

The scope of the constitutionally required parliamentary approval of the appointment of office holders varies from country to country. In some jurisdictions, it involves all diplomatic appointments at ambassadorial level, high court judges, and junior ministers. This is the case in the United States, for instance, which includes the appointment of all federal judges. In other systems such as that in France, parliamentary approval is limited to cabinet ministers who are judged collectively as members of the government of the day. The parliamentary "judgement" is rendered, not so much on the basis of the individual minister's merit as such, as on the program or general policy submitted by the Prime Minister and his cabinet. The same is true in Britain and other parliamentary systems.

Parliamentary approval of Presidential appointment of office holders under the Eritrean constitution system, which is a compromise system uniquely combining aspects of the presidential and parliamentary systems, is appropriately limited to those listed above. All are high positions of crucial importance to the nation covering various aspects of its life. The case of the ministers needs no explanation as they collectively represent extensive authority. The approval of this appointment is the first "line of defense" in Parliament's role in the system of checks and balances. The case of the Commissioners is similar to that of ministers;

apart from the fact of their non-membership of the Cabinet, they perform functions that are as important as those of ministerial functions. To take the example of the Commissioner of Elections, he/she is, as was noted before, the repository of the trust of the nation in election matters who is entrusted with guaranteeing the integrity of the electoral process. Such an office holder must necessarily be appointed with the approval of Parliament. The same is true with the Auditor-General, the Governor of the National Bank and the Chief Justice and Justices of the Supreme Court.

V. Parliamentary Process

Parliamentary life is defined by parliamentary process. The process itself is measured by rules of procedure governing the internal institutions that comprise Parliament and the dynamics of their operation, as well as their relationship with the Executive branch of government. For the purpose of analysis and exposition, we will leave to the next section the question of parliamentary privileges and immunities, although these latter impinge on the quality of the institutional life of Parliament, including the behavior or performances of its members.

In terms of the Eritrean Constitution, Parliament may pass laws or resolutions and undertake such measures as are necessary to discharge its constitutional responsibilities. The internal institutions--the standing and ad hoc committees--that Parliament creates and the rules on procedure that it lays down, are designed to enable it to discharge its constitutional responsibilities and to exercise its powers. The Constitution provides the basis for the accomplishment of these tasks and for the resolution of any potential conflicts that may arise in Parliament's performance of its duties or the exercise of its power.

Parliamentary rules of Procedure

Article 36 of the Constitution lays down, in broad outline, the rules under which the National assembly (Parliament) is required to have regular session and is authorized to determine the timing and duration of its regular session. [36(1). The National Assembly issues "rules and regulations concerning the organization, tasks and the organization of the standing and ad hoc committees and its Secretariat, as well as the rules governing the code of conduct of its members and transparency of its operations." (36(5).

Constitutional Amendment (Article 59)

The Constitution of Eritrea lays down a two-step procedure for constitutional amendment, following a proposal tabled for such an amendment. The initial proposal for amendment of any provision of the Constitution may be tabled by the President or 50 percent of all members of the National Assembly. [59(1)]

The amendment proposal will then be debated by all the members of the National Assembly, and if three-quarters of all the members vote in favor of the amendment, the matter will be put on record and await final disposal by Parliament the following year. A one-year period must elapse before the matter is taken up again. If a year later, four-fifth of all the members accept the amendment passed by a three-fourth majority the previous year, then the amendment will pass and on the effective **date** become a part of the Constitution. [Article 59(2)]

State of Emergency

Parliament may be convened for emergency meeting at the request of the President, by a Proclamation published in the Official Gazette. (Article 27(1). But such a declaration shall not become effective unless approved by a two-thirds majority of all its members of the National Assembly (27(2). A declaration approved by the National Assembly shall continue in force for a period of six months after the approval, and it may be extended for three months. (27(3).s.

Note the following 3 points

1. The most common occurrence in respect of emergency meeting, as illustrated by the experience of other countries, is one in

which the President convenes Parliament in terms of the circumstances stipulated I Article 26 of the Constitution of Eritrea. Very rarely, the Chairman or members may request such a meeting particularly in the event of political crises facing the nation in which the President is either unable or unwilling to call a meeting.
2. The National assembly may, at any time, by resolution revoke a declaration approved by it pursuant to the provisions of Article 27.
3. A declaration of a state of emergency or any measure undertaken, or laws enacted pursuant to it **shall not**:
    a. suspend Articles 14(1)and (2); 16; 17(2); and 19(1) of the Constitution.

[The authot advises all readers to consult with the provisions of the constitution listed in a above].

Another point worth noting in relation to parliamentary rules of procedure which has been included in the Constitution concerns the approval of a draft law passed by Parliament. The Constitution's provision is simple: "Any draft law approved by the National Assembly", it says, "shall be transmitted to the President who, within thirty days period, shall sign and have published in the Gazette of Eritrean Laws." [Article 33]

During the research and subsequent discussion phases of the Constitutional Commission's work this question was among those many others that were hotly debated. It was debated in relation to the larger question: What form of government would be suitable for Eritrea?

The approval procedure of a draft law and related rules in presidential systems is different from that under parliamentary system. In a presidential system with a strict separation of powers, the president may reject a parliamentary draft law. When that occurs, rules must be devised constitutionally to resolve the conflict. Under the US Constitution, a presidential veto of a draft law passed by Congress (Parliament) will "kill" the draft unless Congress overrides the veto by a two-thirds majority. In parliamentary systems, with a single Chamber, all that is required is a majority of votes in the Chamber supporting the party in power. But this may be complicated where, in a Parliament elected under proportional representation, there are a number of parties whose total votes may outnumber those of the principal party. Moreover, in a two-Chamber Parliament the process may be further complicated in the event of a split in the votes that may necessitate a joint session of both Chambers to settle the split. [50]

In the Eritrean situation, which is a parliamentary system with an executive President, a draft law passed by Parliament cannot be questioned or returned for review; it must be published as law. This constitutional requirement should be understood in the context of the Executive's initiative in preparing law. In the vast majority of cases, it is the Executive that proposes laws to be enacted by the Legislature.

VI. CONCLUSION

This essay began with a brief discussion of the idea of democracy as a source of parliamentary (representative) government. Needless to say, parliamentary government *per se* does not a democracy make, although it is a critical dimension in institutional terms. In the democratic system, Parliament, by whatever name it is known, is the primary institution accountable to the citizens of a country, in theory--in the dialectic of the ruler and the ruled. There is an inherent tension in that dialectic even in the best of circumstances, and the citizens' representatives are--or should be--the first line of defense for the rights of their constituents. Democracy and electoral politics are thus critically linked to the role of Parliament in a constitutional government.

But constitutional government does not function in a vacuum. As already noted, the overall historical context--the economic condition, the social milieu and cultural heritage of the country, as well as the political environment--combine to influence the outcome of the democratic process. Moreover, there is the role of leadership; in the dynamic interaction of principle and practice, in any historical context, the role of leadership is critical. A wise and able leadership looks beyond advantages of the moment, into the future. Such a leadership also endeavors to instill and maintain respect for the law--for a government of law, as against a "government of men."

During the extensive public consultation of Eritrea's constitution making process of 1994-1997, these points--leadership and the imperative of a government of law-- were among the most frequently raised and debated. Most people expressed concerns centered on three basic issues: (1) government accountability and transparency, (2) the need for multi-parties to ensure these, and (3) economic policy.

The first and second concerns are answered by the Constitution which guarantees them. With respect to the third-- economic policy-- the governing party of the country, the governing party of Eritrea The People's Front for Democracy and Justice (PFDJ), considers rapid economic growth as an overriding priority, and it has expressed serious doubts as to whether a multi-party system would work at the present. The priority goal of rapid growth as well as the stability required for such growth and for good governance in general. The truth is that there has been neither growth nor stability. The wrong policy and disastrous politics have denied the claim of any substance. It remains to be seen if a change of regime might release the captive native genius to be aroused arise and flourish.

www.ingramcontent.com/pod-product-compliance
Lightning Source LLC
Chambersburg PA
CBHW020658220526
45464CB00001B/484